Self-Defense Against Knife /

Warning

This book contains, in part, techniques that could be dangerous and they should only be carried out under the supervision of a qualified instructor/trainer. The author and the Publishing Company can accept no responsibility for any injury ensuing. All exercises should be carried out with a blunt training-knife (aluminium or wooden). For safety reason, both trainees should wear safety glasses. Due to the risk of injuries, stabs towards the face should not be carried out.

Christian Braun

Self-Defense
Against Knife Attacks

Meyer & Meyer Sport

Original title: Selbstverteidigung gegen Messerangriffe
© Meyer & Meyer Verlag, Aachen, 2006
Translated by Andreas Liebergesell
www.texttransit.com

British Library Cataloguing in Publication Data
A catalogue record for this book is available from the British Library

Christian Braun
Self-Defense Against Knife Attacks
Oxford: Meyer & Meyer Sport (UK) Ltd., 2007
ISBN-10: 1-84126-198-X
ISBN-13: 978-1-84126-198-0

© 2007 by Meyer & Meyer Sport (UK) Ltd.
Aachen, Adelaide, Auckland, Budapest, Graz, Johannesburg, New York,
Olten (CH), Oxford, Singapore, Toronto
Member of the World
Sports Publishers' Association (WSPA)
www.w-s-p-a.org

Printed and bound in Germany by: B.O.S.S Druck und Medien GmbH, Germany
ISBN-10: 1-84126-198-X
ISBN-13: 978-1-84126-198-0
E-Mail: verlag@m-m-sports.com

INDEX

Foreword

Is there an effective self-defense against knife attacks? Does such a thing actually exist? The term "effective" would already disturb an expert, because unarmed defense without injuries is virtually impossible against a practiced knife-fighter. That is obvious to me. Nevertheless, not every attacker is practiced in the use of the weapon and the possibility doesn't always exist to avoid the attack by escaping. Subsequently, I see quite a possibility, in my mind, of increasing the likelihood of surviving an attack.

For approximately 20 years, I have devoted my time to different self-defense systems and have put the most meaningful things together from the various existing systems, and constructed a training program that brings one well in line with this subject.

Which systems do I mean? Basically, the chosen combinations stem from the Kali, Arnis, and Eskrima systems. All these names mean roughly the same. These systems have their seeds in the Philippine Islands and, depending on which of the archipelago is being referred to, one of these terms will be used. In the past, the people of the Philippine Islands have had to resist invaders again and again. And they succeeded well in doing so. Amongst others, the crews of four Spanish men-of-war were slaughtered. The Spanish wore armor and were armed with muskets and swords, and the Philippines were armed only with knifes and cane sticks.

Furthermore, the largest Japanese Katana collection - these are the sharp swords of the Samurai - is to be found on the Philippines. These were taken from the Japanese in battle. Still today, disputes on the islands are sometimes settled with the stick, so that the concepts that have developed over many centuries are very near to the system practiced today. Elements of these systems were also integrated, in the year 2000, into the Ju-Jutsu grading program of the German Ju-Jutsu-Verband, e.V., so that here too one can find further effective concepts in this area.

I have written this book for all those who want to work at the art of self-defense against knife attacks. Essentially, these will be experts and athletes in the martial arts as well as simple beginners, who are interested in this subject.

The book is structured so that first the basic steps are gone through and then step by step each part of the system is presented. There are not only many combinations demonstrated, but also many exercises included. With over 1,700 colored pictures, I hope to show that in the following chapters, everything can be easily understood. Similarly, the program can be used as a basis for training in this area.

I wish the reader lots of enjoyment as you read the book and hope that you never need to use what you have learned.

Frankenthal, July 2005

Christian Braun

Acknowledgements

At this point, above all, I want to thank the trainers with whom I have worked over the past years and with whom I have been able to improve my understanding of weapons. Included in these are: Jeff Espinous, Johan Skalberg, and Timm Blaschke (IKAEF www.ikaef.com). All three are superb experts in the martial arts and are trainers, who are heartily recommended by me.

Furthermore, I also want to thank the following Masters, with whom I have worked both personally or through videos and books (for example). Among these are: Mike Inay, Bob Breen, Dan Inosanto, Marc "Animal" McJung, Joachim Almeria, Paul Vunak, Simone Schloetels, Bernd Hillebrand, Joe (Joachim) Thumfart, and Hock Hochheim.

I also want to thank my students: Robert Zawis, Swen Harz, Gunther Hatzenbühler, and Alexander Emmering; Jessica Rogall (Photography); my girlfriend – Gabi Rogall-Zelt; and my student, friend, and training partner – Waldemar Wodarz for their support of my work.

Dedication

I dedicate this book to my trainers: Jeff Espinous, Johan Skalberg, and Timm Blaschke.

1 Basics - Unarmed Self-defense Against Knife Attacks

Several studies have shown that unarmed defense against someone trained to use a knife can never end up without injuries being inflicted – even though the attacker is up to 20 feet away from you before he attacks!

Therefore, for me, there are three golden rules for unarmed self-defense against knife attacks:

• Get to hell out of it!

• Get to hell out of it!

• Get to hell out of it!

In this case, running away is not cowardly, it's actually rather clever!
Unfortunately, it is not always possible to run away, therefore I want to show the options here that increase the probability of surviving a knife attack. However, the defender should be prepared that he will be injured by the knife. It's now about limiting this injury to a minimum.

In the following, the reader will made aware of the different possibilities for defense against a knife attack. For this, first of all, the natural human reflexes will be used and concepts for effective defense presented. Techniques demanding coordination follow in the secondary step. Drills are used in order to sharpen up the movement sequences. Finally, although possibly injured, a way is shown how one can survive the attack of an expert. Techniques for the different distances: long-distance, short-distance, and for groundwork are also demonstrated.

In principle, at the very first suspicion of a knife attack the defender should cover his throat with his hands, so that a surprise attack will injure the hands and not the throat. To do this, the back of the hands should point towards the attacker, because a cut on the back of the hands is not as dangerous as a cut on the inside of the forearm.

Besides that, the defender should attempt, if possible, to place something between himself and the attacker and therefore gain more time to be able to react. After the successful defense, the defender should get away as quickly as possible and notify the police.

When there are things available that one can use as objects to attack with or to keep one's distance with (e.g. a chair, stick...), the defender should use them. He can also take off his belt and use the buckle to strike back with, or wind his jacket around his arm and use this arm as a shield. He could also take off his shoes, put these over his hands, and ward off the attacker with them.

2   Knife Positions

Generally, I assume here that two knife positions can be used: the dagger/ice pick position (the blade is on the side where the little finger is) and the normal knife position (the blade is on the side where the thumb is). There are other variations besides these two positions, but I do not want to discuss these in further detail here.

3   Attack Angles

According to many of the systems that address themselves to self-defense against knife attacks, the first five angles of attack are identical. These and others will be presented in the following lessons. Essentially, Attack Angles 1-5 will be the ones covered in this book.

For the Angles 1-4, it doesn't matter if the knife is in the normal knife or dagger position. For Angle 5 it does make a difference. When the knife is held in the knife position (blade is on the thumb side), it is possible to strike and also stab.

As a rule, all attacks should not only be executed with the right hand, but also with the left. This applies for all combinations and exercises described in this book.

Angle No. 1 (Knife strike/stab coming in downwards and inwards from the outside at the neck)

The strike/stab is carried out from the right downwards and inwards from the outside at the left side of D's neck.

Angle No. 2 (Knife strike/stab coming in downwards and outwards from the inside at the neck)

The strike/stab is carried out from the left downwards and outwards from the inside at the right side of D's neck.

Angle No. 3 (Knife strike/stab from the outside inwards at waist level)

The strike/stab is carried out from the right at hip height horizontally at the left side of D's upper body (hip height).

Angle No. 4 (Knife strike/stab from the inside towards the outside at waist level)

The strike/stab is carried out from the left at hip height horizontally at the right side of D's upper body (hip height).

Angle No. 5 (Knife stab at the stomach)

Normal knife position: The stab is carried out directly at D's stomach.
Dagger position: The stab is carried out vertically downwards at D's head / upper body.

4   Forms of Attack

- Stab – The knifepoint penetrates deeply into the body

- Strike – Slitting the skin

- Chop attack – Hacking or whacking with the knife, e.g. with the blade against the extremities

- Slashing – Short and quick action with the knife in order to cause a lot of small wounds

5   Possible Injuries

A stab causes a small entry wound in the body that can still be very deep. When the knife injures internal organs, it can be life-threatening for the victim.

With a strike, the skin is cut open to a greater or lesser degree. When this happens in a sensitive area, such as the throat or the inside of the forearm, it can also be highly life-threatening.

The chop attack would be, for example, used against extremities, when the defender wants to execute an attack. Here also, depending upon the point of contact (e.g. the inner forearm), this can be life-threatening.

When a defender suffers lots of slashes, as a rule, his many wounds will cause him, sooner or later to surrender. When the cuts are made at a vital point (neck, inside of the wrist), a threat to life also arises.

No presumption should be made here about which is the most dangerous type of attack. Irrespective of which vital-points are injured, such as the neck, the inner forearms, the groin, the shoulders or also internal organs, an absolute life-threatening danger will exist.

6   First Aid for Injuries

Stabbing or cutting injuries can be life-threatening. Therefore a few hints follow here as they are taught on different first aid courses.

In principle, a first aid helper should not extract a knife that is stuck in a body, because by doing so the wound could bleed more strongly. The wound should be wrapped with bandages around the knife.

Cutting injuries should be covered with bandages, or when necessary, a compression bandage should be applied. If parts of the body have been severed, a compression bandage is to be applied and the detached body-parts stored in a bag, which, where possible should then be stored in a second bag that contains ice.

Afterwards, it is important that the victim is brought as fast as possible to a hospital. If possible, the time of the injury (severance) should be noted, so that this piece of information is available to the doctors at the hospital. An ambulance should transport the victim, since it is possible that the victim may suffer a shock on the way to the hospital and that the driver cannot give him the necessary care. Also, the traffic situation could prevent a fast trip to the hospital.

More detailed information over first aid measures can be obtained from the appropriate organizations responsible, such as the Red Cross.

7 Tips for Training

- First, only the technical sequence should be practiced. Here, the partner offers no resistance. Only when everything begins to become natural should the partner offer resistance (70%) in order to see whether the technique works.

- The learned techniques should be "tried out" on somebody, who is technically not as good (a beginner with some experience) and lighter. Here, one can use what has been learned without being confronted with effective counter-techniques. If the partner is more experienced, and maybe also stronger, the danger exists that one will consider the new techniques as ineffective, because they cannot be applied, and no longer practices them.

- When a technique doesn't succeed in training, because one doesn't understand the movements, it can be advisable to make a short pause, for example get something to drink or go to the toilet. In this case, a block between the two halves of the brain may be the cause of confusion. Both halves of the brain have their own function. With many people, the left half of the brain controls the functions of: logic, analysis, speech, numbers, linearity and others. The right half of the brain is responsible for rhythm, area-perception, fantasy, etc. In order to complete an exercise sequence, both halves of the brain must work together. In stressful situations or with overload (which can also be stressful), it is possible that this is not the case. The legs and arms are crossed during the movements in the exercise sequences, and this action can free up the blockage. This " technique" can also be applied to everyday problems. In the area of kinesiology, there are many exercises that are conducive to both halves of the brain working together better.

- Also the double-stick training in Kali (Arnis and Eskrima) contributes to the improvement of these abilities. When the complex exercises, that require use of both halves of the brain, are often repeated, it can happen that additional connections are formed between both the halves (so-called "synapses"). This then makes it possible for us to perform the exercise sequences more quickly. Studies of the brain have shown, for example, that by performing rhythmic exercise sequences (right half of the brain) the speech process can also be improved (left half of the brain). Thus, the stimulation of the functions of one half of the brain can also benefit the other.

- On the other hand, this pause offers a good opportunity to consider what has been learned and to prepare for what lies ahead. However, these pauses should not be longer than 10 minutes. In order to optimize learning, the first short pause should already take place after approximately 60 minutes of training.

- Shortly after completion of training, the material learned can still be recalled. A day later it is already almost impossible to remember all the details. The ability to remember also has to do with how much interest one has shown in following all of the training. Things, that are very interesting to someone, remain in their memory rather than the things that are not. For this reason, it is advisable that directly after the training the material that has been learned be reviewed (consolidated) and written down. It should be repeated the next day again and, if necessary, supplemented.

- Making notes helps the training to be processed mentally. One way is for the learner to read the description of the technique aloud and visualize the situation, similar to the way used in "shadowboxing." Another method is for the learner to imagine the whole situation. He sees himself in his thoughts – like in a film – in action and lives through the previous day's combinations. One can also record the notes on a cassette or CD and listen to them (for example, while commuting or at home). While one listens to the text, one should envisage the situation as colorfully as possible. So that one can note something especially well, it is advantageous to utilize as many senses as possible simultaneously. With this I mean not only the visual or acoustical senses, but above all also the sense of feeling. Things stay considerably better in my memory if I imagine the effect of a lever or a stranglehold intensively, rather than if I only hear the text. Exaggeration is also a method to remember what has been learned better.

- Positive thinking is necessary in order to be successful. If the trainee becomes negatively influenced before the lesson ("the other person is so big, so awfully strong, and also looks so dangerous..."), he won't often be successful because he has already given up in advance. If a human being positively motivates himself before a task (and that involves not only for sport), it will be considerably much easier for him to reach his goal.

- The setting of goals is also an important point. In order to be successful (and not only for sport) it makes sense to formulate short -, middle -, and long-term goals. These should however be realistic, that is, attainable. One can write the goals on a note and stick it (for example) to the bathroom mirror so that one is constantly reminded. A goal could be: "I will win the next championship."

- Autogenic training helps in the fulfillment of these goals. Here, the trainee always replaces a negative goal with a positive statement (a motto, for example) that he can accept in his subconscious. Wrong would be: "I have no fear." Better: "I can do it!" or: "I am brave." The reason lies in the fact that these formulations are automatically recalled in certain situations. For this area, as for that of mental training, there is an abundance of literature.

- For the purpose of realistic self-defense, from time to time the use of strike techniques should also be practiced in combination with knife attack techniques.

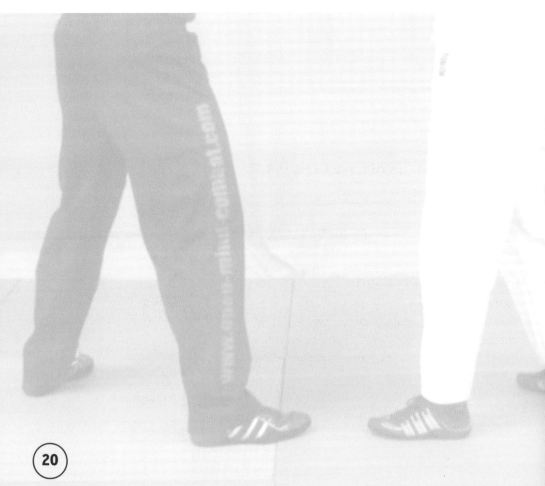

8 Knife Fighting Positions

The positions don't differ essentially from the positions of an unarmed attacker. In principle, the attack can be executed standing or on the ground. The attacker can show the weapon openly, keep it hidden or pull it out during a conflict. In the following section, several positions will be introduced. Seen altogether, the individual positions of the attacker play a less important role.

More important is the position of the defender and the position of his arms. In principle, the duel position (attacker and defender face each other approximately 2 m apart), rarely happens.

A description of the different positions follows. Each position, in which the attacker has a knife in the hand, is very dangerous and can be life-threatening for the person being attacked.

In principle, we distinguish between two positions:

1. The attacker has the knife in front.
2. The attacker has the knife behind his back.

8.1 The Attacker Has the Knife in Front

1

When the attacker holds the knife in front, he is trying to intimidate the defender with it. In order to be able to strike with sufficient energy, the attacker has to draw the knife back. However, he can execute slashes or cuts from this position. In this position, the defender has the possibility to grasp the weapon-bearing arm and work on the attacker with further techniques. You will find further theory about this later in the book.

8.2   Attacker Has the Knife Behind

Here, three positions can be considered:

1.   The knife is directly visible to the defender.

2.   The attacker has hidden the knife (behind his back or thigh for example).

3.   The attacker holds the second hand to shield the knife from being seen.

The attacker can attack from all of these positions with a lot of energy. If he has hidden the knife, on the one hand this makes it difficult for the defender to know the size of the weapon and besides this the attack angle is harder to assess. In this case, the defender should attempt to bring an even greater distance between him and the attacker.

If the attacker puts a hand in front of the knife to shield it, he reckons that defender will try to grasp the weapon-hand. This can be prevented with the free hand. It makes no sense for the defender to grasp the attacker's free hand since it is highly likely that the attacker will immediately injure this hand with the knife.

From each of these positions, the attacker can carry out a feinting attack, change the attack angle and only then stab or strike. This type of attack is very dangerous and very difficult to prevent.

9 Footwork/Theory of Movement

The following theory of movement is taught in many of the Philippine systems:

- Male triangle.
- Female triangle.
- Cat stance

Male triangle
In the male triangle, the angle points towards the attacker. The weight of the body can lie on the forward or the rear foot. In the change over of stance, the rear foot is pulled forward and the front foot is placed to the rear.

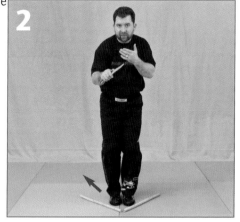

Female triangle

In the female triangle, the angle points towards the defender. The weight of the body can lie on the forwards or on the rear foot. In the change over of stance, the forward foot is pulled to the rear and the rear foot is placed forward.

Cat stance

In the cat stance, 80% of the weight is on the rear leg. The defender stands at an angle of approximately 90° to the attacker.

10 Blocking Techniques

The block techniques should normally be executed so that the little finger side of the hand touches the weapon-bearing arm (Palm down block). This increases the likelihood that injuries received when the attacker withdraws the weapon will be less serious (Photo 1). ☺

The worst situation would be if the defender blocked the weapon-bearing arm with the palm of the hand (Photo 2). If the attacker should then withdraw the knife, the defender's arteries could be severed. A better, but also not optimum variation is when the defender blocks with the back of the hand (Photo 3). However, in this case the gash in the inner arm would also be as wide as the back of the hand. The blocking techniques are normally used if the defender is standing very close to the attacker and a defense using sweeping techniques is not possible.

When attacked, the defender should always execute blocking techniques with the arm closest to the attacker using the natural reflexes. Blocking the weapon-bearing arm diagonally necessitates a great deal of coordination and should only be practiced as a secondary step in training.

11 Sweeping Techniques

The sweeping techniques can be executed with the back of the hand (Photo 1) and with the forehand (Photo 2). For reasons of self-protection, it is also recommended here to sweep the weapon with the back of the hand, so that any injuries the attacker inflicts when withdrawing the knife are less serious. The sweeping techniques can also be applied diagonally, that is, in an attack with the right hand, the defender counters also with the right hand.

This sequence of movements demands a higher level of coordination ability by the defender, because when the arm crosses over the middle line of the body, the other half of the brain is switched in. Not everyone possesses the ability to respond quickly in this situation and must first work at achieving these movements.

12 Use of Blocking or Sweeping Techniques

The use of blocking or sweeping techniques depends on the distance between attacker and defender. The context is explained in the following.

Basic principles for the use of blocking or sweeping techniques:

- Taking on the weapon-bearing arm with the nearer hand, in order to use the natural reflexes.

- In a blocking or sweeping technique, where possible, the palm of the hand is facing towards the ground in order to minimize any possible injuries from the knife.

- The defender should always try to approach the attacker from the outside, since the danger to the person is less in this position than when standing directly in front of the attacker.

13   Reaction Training

1. A holds the knife in the normal position (with the blade on the thumb side) and strikes Angle No. 1 (at D's neck). D carries out a left-handed blocking technique (palm down block). D keeps contact with the weapon-bearing arm.

2. A now switches to Angle No. 3 (at D's hips).
   D carries on 'sticking' to the arm and executes a block with the forearm downwards and outwards.

3. If A uses a lot of pressure, D places his right hand on A's right forearm...

4. ...and carries out a right-handed sweeping action downwards and outwards to the right.

5. A switches now to Angle No. 2 (inwards towards at D's neck).
D keeps on 'sticking' to the arm with his right hand and carries out a block with the forearm downwards to the right.

6. If A uses a lot of pressure, D leads his left hand underneath A's right arm...

7. ...and sweeps the weapon-bearing arm with the left hand outwards to the left.

Start over again...

In a further step the sequence can be carried out freely. The intensity of training can be increased if D is blindfolded and has to react only to his tactile feelings.

14   Distances

As generally the case in any self-defense system, there are different distances in the area of the defense against weapons.

Long-range (Largo Mano)
The attacker is not able to touch the defender with the weapon in his outstretched hand.

Medium Range (Sumbrada Range)
The attacker is able to touch the defender's nose with the weapon in his outstretched hand.

Close Range (Trapping Range)
The attacker is able to touch the defender's ear with the weapon in his outstretched hand.

Throwing/Groundwork Range (Grappling Range)

The attacker is able to touch the defender's neck with the weapon in his outstretched hand.

15 Actions Applicable to the Different Distances

- Interception
- Dodging/Feinting
- Striking/Gunting
- Sweeping
- Blocking
- Blocking and Punching or Kicking techniques
- Grappling
- Grappling and Punching or Kicking techniques

15.1 Interception ☺

The most effective way to overcome an attack without an injury is to have the drop on the attacker (Interception). This action can be used in every distance. If the attacker clearly indicates that he is about to attack or is even perhaps already visibly holding a weapon in his hand, the defender can make use of his right of self-defense because the attack is in place and is illegal. The defender should immediately carry out an effective technique against one of the attacker's vital points (eyes, nose, larynx or genitalia).

Exercise

A is holding the knife in the normal position and brings it into one of the Attack Angles (Photo 1). D now takes a lunging step forwards while at the same time delivering a finger jab at A's eyes (Photo 2).

In this exercise, it is advisable to strike with the fingers at A's forehead to prevent an injury of the eyes, while at the same time exercising the proper training for the distance.

15.2 Dodging/Feinting

A dodging or feinting maneuver is mainly used in the long-range distances.

Exercise
A holds the knife in the normal position and strikes using Angles No. 1-5 (Photo 1).
D simply carries out a dodging maneuver (Photo 1).

Angle 1

Angle 2

Angle 3

Angle 4

Angle 5

15.3 Striking/Gunting

In this situation both the attacker and defender are at long or medium range distance. Depending on whether the defender also has a knife for defending, he strikes the attacking arm or chops down on it (Gunting - term meaning 'scissors'). By using a gunting chop (striking at vital points) you can hurt the attacker. As soon as the defender realizes that the attacker is suffering pain, this gives the opportunity for further actions to be taken against him.

Exercise
A holds the knife in the normal position and strikes using Angles No. 1-5 (Photo 1). If D has a knife to defend himself with, he slashes the hand or forearm of the attacking weapon-bearing arm (Photo 2). If D doesn't have a knife, he strikes downwards with his knuckles at A's weapon-bearing hand.

Angle 1

Angle 2

Angle 3

Angle 4

Angle 5

15.4 Sweeping

D mainly uses the sweeping techniques in the medium (sumbrada) range. Whenever possible, D sweeps the weapon-bearing hand sideways with the back of the hand or the little finger side of the hand.

Exercise

A holds the knife in the normal position and strikes using Angles No. 1-5 (Photo 1). D sweeps the weapon-bearing arm away (Photo 2-3). As he does this, the free hand protects the neck. D carries out the sweeping action with the back of the hand or the little finger side of the hand.

Angle 1

Angle 2

Angle 3

Angle 4

Angle 5: Variation 1

Variation 2 ☺

15.5 Blocking

A holds the knife in the normal position and strikes using Angles No. 1-5. D is in close (trapping) range. In this situation it is difficult to sweep the weapon-bearing arm sideways. D blocks the attack with the nearest arm.

Exercise
A holds the knife in the normal position and strikes using Angles No. 1-5 (Photo 1). D blocks the attack with the arm nearest to the weapon-bearing arm (Photo 2).

Angle 1

Angle 2

Angle 3

Angle 4

Angle 5

15.6   Blocking and Punching or Kicking Techniques

A holds the knife in the normal position and strikes using Angles No. 1-5. D is in close (trapping) range. Thus it is difficult to sweep the weapon-bearing arm sideways. D blocks the attack with the nearest arm. At the same time, he carries out a punching technique with the free hand or a kicking technique with one of his legs.

Exercise

A holds the knife in the normal position and strikes using Angles No. 1-5 (Photo 1). D blocks the attack with the arm nearest to the weapon-bearing arm and delivers a finger jab at the eyes with the free hand or uses a foot technique (foot kick, shinbone kick, stamping kick) at A's legs or genitalia (Photo 2).

Angle 1

Angle 2

Angle 3

Angle 4

Angle 5

15.7   Grabbing

A holds the knife in the normal position and strikes using Angles No. 1-5. D is in close (trapping) range. Thus, it is difficult to sweep the weapon-bearing arm sideways. With both hands, D grabs hold of the attacking arm and controls it this way.

Exercise

A holds the knife in the normal position and strikes using Angles No. 1-5 (Photo 1). With both hands, D grabs hold of the weapon-bearing arm (controlling it) (Photo 2).

Angle 1

Angle 2

Angle 3

Angle 4

Angle 5

15.8 Grabbing and Punching or Kicking Techniques

A holds the knife in the normal position and strikes using Angles No. 1-5. D is in close (trapping) range. Thus, it is difficult to sweep the weapon-bearing arm sideways. D grabs hold of the attacking arm with both hands (controlling the weapon-bearing arm) and then carries out a kicking technique or other punching techniques or a head butt.

Exercise
A holds the knife in the normal position and strikes using Angles No. 1-5 (Photo 1). With both hands, D grabs hold of the weapon-bearing arm and then carries out a kicking technique at the legs or genitalia. Following on from this a punching technique or a head butt could be used (Photo 2).

Angle 1

Angle 2

Angle 3

Angle 4

Angle 5

All the exercises can be expanded in the following ways:

- By taking a step forwards/backwards:
  When A takes a step forwards, D simultaneously takes a step backwards and vice versa.

- Free play (the partner only strikes Attack Angles 1-5 and, otherwise, remains passive):
  A and D carry out a form of sparring in which A's actions are limited to carrying out Attack Angles 1-5. Both, A and D, move freely around. According to the distance, D uses one of the exercises presented here. A simply dodges back or forwards in order to alter his distance from D.

- As a complex exercise:
  A strikes with Attack Angles 1-5 one after the other. Both of them move around freely. According to the distance, D uses one of the exercises presented here. Otherwise, A remains passive. His function can be compared to a ball machine at the tennis-court.

16 Defense against Knife Attacks by Controlling the Weapon-bearing Arm

In this section, the focus is on controlling the weapon-bearing arm. Disarming and disrupting techniques are described in detail in the grading programs (brown and black belt).

Here, a system is taught that makes it possible for the pupil to be able to learn these techniques fairly quickly. All defense actions are based on the following common principles:

- Blocking is done using the nearest hand in order to make use of the natural reflexes.

- If, after carrying out the block, D is standing on the inside, he moves to the outside.

- If, after carrying out the block, D is standing on the outside, he stays outside.

- The palm of the hand is always pointing towards the ground in order to avoid serious knife injuries when the knife is pulled back.

www.open-mind-combat.com

16.1 Angle No. 1 (Knife strike in downwards and inwards from the outside at the neck)

1. A strikes using Angle No. 1 (downwards and inwards from the outside at the neck).
2. Using the three-step contact, D carries out a block with the left arm...
3. ...and a sweeping action outwards with the right arm...
4. ... – controlling with the left – to sweep A's weapon-bearing arm outwards to the right.
5. D's left hand is placed underneath A's elbow and the right hand is placed directly on top of the elbow.
    With a right-handed finger jab, D threatens A's right eye. Pressure on the weapon-bearing arm is applied towards A's left shoulder so that a strike using the left hand is no longer possible.

16.2 Angle No. 2 (Knife strike downwards and outwards from the inside at the neck)

1. A strikes using Angle No. 2 (from the inside at the neck).
2. D blocks the weapon-bearing arm with his right hand.
3. D's left hand is placed underneath A's elbow...
4. ...and the right hand is placed directly on top of the elbow.
With a right-handed finger jab, D threatens A's right eye.
Pressure on the weapon-bearing arm is applied towards A's left shoulder so that a strike using the left hand is no longer possible.

16.3 Angle No. 3 (Knife strike from the outside at waist level)

1. A strikes using Angle No. 3 (from the outside at waist level).
2. Using the three-step contact, D carries out a block downwards and outwards with the left arm...
3. ...and a sweeping action outwards with the right arm...
4. ...– controlling with the left – to sweep A's weapon-bearing arm outwards to the right.
5. D's left hand is placed underneath A's elbow and the right hand is placed directly on top of the elbow. With a right-handed finger jab, D threatens A's right eye. Pressure on the weapon-bearing arm is applied towards A's left shoulder so that a strike using the left hand is no longer possible.

16.4 Angle No. 4 (Knife strike from the inside towards the outside at waist level)

1. A strikes using Angle No. 4 (from the inside towards the outside at waist level).
2. D blocks the weapon-bearing arm with his right hand.
3. D's left hand is placed underneath A's elbow...
4. ...and the right hand is placed directly on top of the elbow.
   With a right-handed finger jab, D threatens A's right eye.
   Pressure on the weapon-bearing arm is applied towards A's left shoulder so that a strike using the left hand is no longer possible.

16.5   Angle No. 5 (Knife stab at the stomach)

1.   A stabs using Angle No. 5 (at the stomach).
2.   D blocks the weapon-bearing arm with his right hand.
3.   D's left hand is placed underneath A's elbow...
4.   ...and the right hand is placed directly on top of the elbow.
     With a right-handed finger jab, D threatens A's right eye.
     Pressure on the weapon-bearing arm is applied towards A's left shoulder so that a strike using the left hand is no longer possible.

16.6 Simplification

When these techniques have been mastered, the following can be adapted for use in combination with Attack Angles No. 1 and 3:

1. A strikes using Angle No. 1 (inwards from the outside at the neck).

2. D carries out a sweeping block with the right hand counter-clockwise downwards and outwards...

3. ...places the left hand underneath A's elbow...

4. ...and the right hand directly on top of A's elbow.

5. With a right-handed finger jab, D threatens A's right eye.
Pressure on the weapon-bearing arm is applied towards A's left shoulder so that a strike using the left hand is no longer possible.

With this combination you can "save" one action, but it makes greater demands on coordination and should be practiced first of all during the secondary step of training.

16.7   Training Method

Phase 1

1. A is standing behind D with a knife in his hand.
   A calls out which attack angle he will use and gives D time to work out which combination he will reply with (4-5 seconds).
2. When A says "NOW", D turns round.
3. A now executes the attack he has announced. With the left hand D carries out an edge of the hand block (Palm down block) upwards and outwards...
4. ...places the right forearm on top of A's right forearm

5. ...and sweeps A's right arm downwards and outwards to the right...
6. ...controls A's right elbow with the left hand ...
7. ...places the right arm on top of A's right elbow (this combination is called 'hammer and anvil') and with a right-handed finger threatens to jab A's eyes.

Phase 2

D keeps his eyes closed all the time and, to start with, A reduces the speed of the attack. This form of mental training is called ideomotor training. It is scientifically proven that you improve your skills by this form of training. Also competitive athletes in other disciplines utilize this form of training.

17 Defense against Knife Attacks using Disrupting Techniques

In this section, the focus is on disrupting techniques. With the aid of these disrupting techniques you can inflict pain upon A so that D gains time to execute his combination. A cannot react for a couple of seconds due to his dazed state of shock. It is also possible to execute the disrupting techniques in such a manner (e.g. finger jab at the eyes or at the larynx) that A is completely immobilized and therefore further action will be unnecessary.

Here, a system is taught that makes it possible for the pupil to be able to learn these techniques fairly quickly. All the types of defense are based on the following common principles:

* Blocking is done using the nearest hand in order to make use of the natural reflexes.

* If, after carrying out the block, D is standing on the inside, he moves to the outside.

* If, after carrying out the block, D is standing on the outside, he stays outside.

* The palm of the hand is always pointing towards the ground in order to avoid serious knife injuries when the knife is pulled back.

As far as possible, the first combination is the same for every attack angle. This has been done on purpose to show that you need only use one sequence of movements for all five attack angles.

17.1 Angle No. 1 (Knife strike coming in downwards and inwards from the outside at the neck)

1. A strikes using Angle No. 1 (inwards from the outside at the neck)
2. With his left forearm, D carries out a block outwards, while at the same time delivering a right-handed finger jab (disrupting technique) at A's eyes.
3. D leads his right arm over A's weapon-bearing arm...
4. ...and carries out a sweeping action against the arm downwards and outwards to the right.
5. D places his left hand underneath A's right elbow...
6. ...and places his right arm over A's right arm. The finger tips of his right hand point towards A's face.

   Pressure on the weapon-bearing arm is applied towards A's left shoulder so that a strike using the left hand is no longer possible.

1. A strikes using Angle No. 1 (inwards from the outside at the neck).

2. With his left forearm, D carries out a block outwards, while at the same time delivering a blow with his right elbow (disrupting technique) to A's right biceps.

3. D leads his right arm over A's weapon-bearing arm...

4. ...and carries out a sweeping action against the arm downwards and outwards to the right.

5. D places his left hand underneath A's right elbow...

6. ...and places his right arm over A's right arm. The finger tips of his right hand point towards A's face. Pressure on the weapon-bearing arm is applied towards A's left shoulder so that a strike using the left hand is no longer possible.

1. A strikes using Angle No. 1 (inwards from the outside at the neck)
2. With his left forearm, D carries out a block outwards, while at the same time delivering a right-handed punch (disrupting technique) to A's right shoulder.
3. D leads his right arm over A's weapon-bearing arm ...
4. ...and carries out a sweeping action against the arm downwards and outwards to the right.
5. D places his left hand underneath A's right elbow and places his right arm over A's right arm. The fingertips of his right hand point towards A's face.
6. Pressure on the weapon-bearing arm is applied towards A's left shoulder so that a strike using the left hand is no longer possible.

17.2 Angle No. 2 (Knife strike downwards and outwards from the inside at the neck)

1. A strikes using Angle No. 2 (from the inside at the neck).
2. With his right forearm, D blocks A's weapon-bearing arm, while at the same time delivering a left-handed finger jab (disrupting technique) at A's eyes.
3. D places his left hand underneath A's elbow...
4. ...and the right hand is placed directly on top of A's elbow.
   D threatens A's right eye with a right-handed finger jab.
   Pressure on the weapon-bearing arm is applied towards A's left shoulder so that a strike using the left hand is no longer possible.

1. A strikes using Angle No. 2 (from the inside at the neck).

2. With his right hand, D blocks A's weapon-bearing arm, while at the same time delivering a blow with his left elbow (disrupting technique) to A's upper arm. With the fingers of his right hand he secures A's right wrist so that it cannot be easily pulled back.

3. D places his left hand underneath A's elbow...

4. ...and the right hand is placed directly on top of A's elbow.
   D threatens A's right eye with a right-handed finger jab.
   Pressure on the weapon-bearing arm is applied towards A's left shoulder so that a strike using the left hand is no longer possible.

1. A strikes using Angle No. 2 (from the inside at the neck).
2. With his right hand, D blocks A's weapon-bearing arm, while at the same time delivering a blow with his outstretched left upper arm (disrupting technique in the form of an armbreaker) to A's right upper arm. With the fingers of his right hand he secures A's right wrist so that it cannot be easily pulled back.
3. D places his left hand underneath A's elbow and the right hand is placed directly on top of A's elbow.
4. D threatens A's right eye with a right-handed finger jab.
   Pressure on the weapon-bearing arm is applied towards A's left shoulder so that a strike using the left hand is no longer possible.

17.3   Angle No. 3 (Knife strike from the outside at waist level)

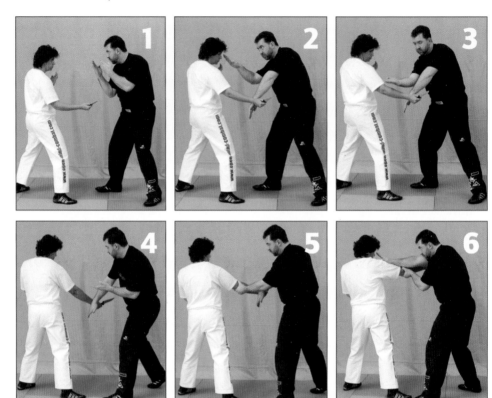

1.   A strikes using Angle No. 3 (from the outside at waist level).
2.   With his left forearm, D carries out a block downwards and outwards, while at the same time delivering a right-handed finger jab (disrupting technique) at A's eyes.
3.   D leads his right arm over A's weapon-bearing arm...
4.   ...and carries out a sweeping action against the arm downwards and outwards to the right.
5.   D places his left hand underneath A's right elbow...
6.   ...and places his right arm over A's right arm. The finger tips of his right hand point towards A's face.
     Pressure on the weapon-bearing arm is applied towards A's left shoulder so that a strike using the left hand is no longer possible.

1. A strikes using Angle No. 3 (from the outside at waist level).
2. With his left forearm, D carries out a block downwards and outwards, while at the same time delivering a blow with his right elbow (disrupting technique) to A's right biceps.
3. D leads his right arm over A's weapon-bearing arm...
4. ...and carries out a sweeping action against the arm downwards and outwards to the right.
5. D places his left hand underneath A's right elbow...
6. ...and places his right arm over A's right arm. The finger tips of his right hand point towards A's face. Pressure on the weapon-bearing arm is applied towards A's left shoulder so that a strike using the left hand is no longer possible.

1. strikes using Angle No. 3 (from the outside at waist level).

2. With his left forearm, D carries out a block downwards and outwards, while at the same time delivering a right-handed punch (disrupting technique) to A's right shoulder.

3. D leads his right arm over A's weapon-bearing arm...

4. ...and carries out a sweeping action against the arm downwards and outwards to the right.

5. D places his left hand underneath A's right elbow...

6. ...and places his right arm over A's right arm. The finger tips of his right hand point towards A's face.
   Pressure on the weapon-bearing arm is applied towards A's left shoulder so that a strike using the left hand is no longer possible.

17.4 Angle No. 4 (Knife strike from the inside at waist level)

1. A strikes using Angle No. 4 (from the inside at waist level).
2. With his right hand, D blocks A's weapon-bearing arm downwards and outwards, while at the same time delivering a left-handed finger jab (disrupting technique) at A's eyes.
3. D places his left hand underneath A's elbow...
4. ...and the right hand is placed directly on top of A's elbow.
   D threatens A's right eye with a right-handed finger jab.
   Pressure on the weapon-bearing arm is applied towards A's left shoulder so that a strike using the left hand is no longer possible.

1. A strikes using Angle No. 4 (from the inside at waist level).

2. With his right hand, D blocks A's weapon-bearing arm downwards and outwards, while at the same time delivering a blow with his left elbow (disrupting technique) to A's right upper arm. With his right hand he secures A's right wrist so that it cannot be easily pulled back.

3. D places his left hand underneath A's elbow...

4. ...and the right hand is placed directly on top of A's elbow.
D threatens A's right eye with a right-handed finger jab.
Pressure on the weapon-bearing arm is applied towards A's left shoulder so that a strike using the left hand is no longer possible.

1. A strikes using Angle No. 4 (from the inside at waist level).

2. With his right hand, D blocks A's weapon-bearing arm downwards and outwards, while at the same time delivering a blow with his outstretched left upper arm (disrupting technique in the form of an armbreaker) to A's right upper arm. With the fingers of his right hand, D secures A's right wrist so that it cannot be easily pulled back.

3. D places his left hand underneath A's elbow...

4. ...and the right hand is placed directly on top of A's elbow.
D threatens A's right eye with a right-handed finger jab.
Pressure on the weapon-bearing arm is applied towards A's left shoulder so that a strike using the left hand is no longer possible.

17.5 Attack No. 5 (Knife stab at the stomach)

1. A stabs using Angle No. 5 (at the stomach).
2. With his right hand, D blocks A's weapon-bearing arm downwards and outwards, while at the same time delivering a left-handed finger jab (disrupting technique) at A's eyes.
3. D places his left hand underneath A's elbow...
4. ...and the right hand is placed directly on top of A's elbow.
    D threatens A's right eye with a right-handed finger jab.
    Pressure on the weapon-bearing arm is applied towards A's left shoulder so that a strike using the left hand is no longer possible.

1. A stabs using Angle No. 5 (at the stomach).
2. With his left hand, D carries out a sweeping action inwards, while at the same time delivering a blow with his right elbow (disrupting technique) at A's right upper arm.
3. With his right hand, D grabs hold of A's right wrist...
4. ...places his left hand underneath A's elbow...
5. ...and the right hand directly on top of A's elbow. D threatens A's right eye with a right-handed finger jab. Pressure on the weapon-bearing arm is applied towards A's left shoulder so that a strike using the left hand is no longer possible.

1. A stabs using Angle No. 5 (at the stomach).

2. With his left hand, D blocks A's weapon-bearing arm downwards and outwards, while at the same time delivering a right-handed punch (disrupting technique) to A's right shoulder.

3. D places his right forearm on top of A's right forearm...

4. ...carries out a sweeping action with his right arm against A's right arm outwards to the right...

5. ...places his left hand underneath A's elbow...

6. ...and the right hand directly on top of A's elbow. D threatens A's right eye with a right-handed finger jab. Pressure on the weapon-bearing arm is applied towards A's left shoulder so that a strike using the left hand is no longer possible.

17.6   Simplification

When these techniques have been mastered, the following can be adapted for use in combination with Attack No.'s 1 and 3:

1. A strikes using Angle No. 1 (inwards from the outside at the neck).
2. D places his right forearm on top of A's right forearm, while at the same time delivering a left-handed finger jab (disrupting technique) at A's eyes...
3. ...and carries out a sweeping action against the weapon carrying arm downwards and outwards to the right.
4. D places his left hand underneath A's elbow
5. ...and the right hand directly on top of A's elbow.
    D threatens A's right eye with a right-handed finger jab.
    Pressure on the weapon-bearing arm is applied towards A's left shoulder so that a strike using the left hand is no longer possible.

With this combination you can "save" one action, but it makes greater demands on coordination and should be practiced first of all in the secondary step of training.

17.7 Training Method

Phase 1

1. A is standing in front of D with a knife in his hand. A calls out which attack angle he will use and gives D time to work out which combination he will reply with (4-5 seconds). When A says "NOW" D opens his eyes...

2. ...and A executes the attack he has announced.

3. D blocks with the nearest arm, in order to make use of the natural reflexes, while at the same time delivering a finger jab at A's eyes and moves to or stays outside. D places his right forearm on top of A's right forearm...

4. ...carries out a sweeping action against the arm downwards and outwards to the right...

5. ...places his left hand underneath A's right elbow...

6. ...and the right arm directly on top of A's elbow.

Phase 2

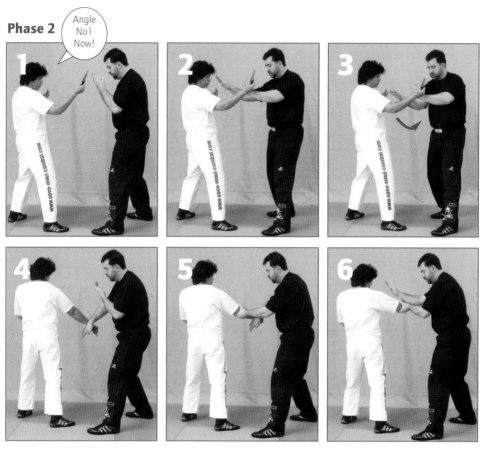

The sequence is the same as in Phase 1, but D keeps his eyes closed all the time and to start with A reduces the speed of the attack.

Phase 3

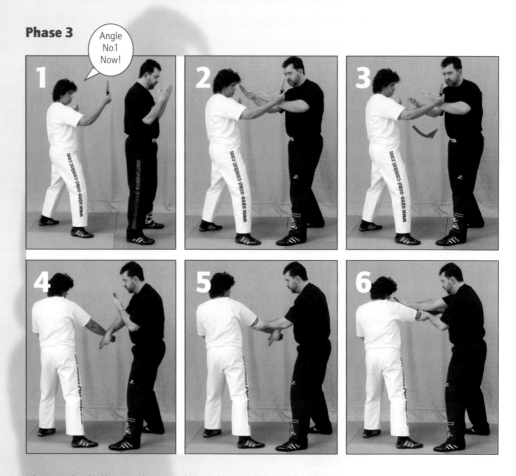

Phase 3 is similar to Phase 2, but A is standing behind D.
When A says "NOW" D turns around.

18 Defense Against Knife Attacks Using Disarming Techniques

To a large extent, the first combination is the same for every attack angle. This has been done on purpose to show that you need only use one sequence of movements for all five attack angles.

18.1 Examples of Disarming Techniques

- With the hand
- With the edge of the hand
- With the forearm
- Using the upper arm
- Using the thigh
- By a punching technique on the weapon-bearing arm/hand
- Using the attacker's body

18.2 Methods of Securing the Weapon after a Successful Disarming Action

Where the disarming action is done with the hand, the defender has secured the weapon and can make use of it to defend himself with, or he can simply secure it as evidence. Should the weapon fall on the ground, it is not always a wise thing to try to pick it up straight away and secure it. If, in a defensive situation, one is surrounded by many people, it could be dangerous to bend down to pick up the weapon.

One of the people could start a sudden attack. In this case it is better to stand on the weapon. Thus, it is safe, i.e., others cannot use it and the defender does not run the risk of being caught by surprise when bending down. Should the attacker go away, the weapon should be kept under the defender's shoe or foot until it is safe to bend down.

18.3 Angle No. 1 (Knife strike downwards and inwards from the outside at the neck)

1. A strikes using Angle No. 1 (inwards from the outside at the neck).

2. D carries out an edge of the hand block upwards and outwards to the left, while at the same time delivering a right-handed finger jab (disrupting technique) at the head and taking a lunging step 45° forwards to the right.

3. D leads his right arm underneath A's right arm...

4. ...moves the weapon-bearing arm clockwise to the right with his right hand...

5. ...and then further downwards until the tip of the knife points at the ground while placing his right leg one step backwards. The right hand grabs hold of A's ball of the thumb...

6. ...places the right hand (with the palm of the hand facing upwards) directly underneath A's right hand...

7. ...and disarms A using the left hand (with the palm of the left hand facing upwards).

1.   A strikes using Angle No. 1 (inwards from the outside at the neck).
2.   D places his right forearm on top of A's right forearm, while at the same time delivering a left-handed finger jab (disrupting technique) at A's eyes...
3.   ... with his right hand he leads the weapon-bearing arm diagonally downwards and outwards to the right...
4.   ...grabs hold of the ball of A's right thumb with his left hand ...
5.   ...places the right forearm on the flat, blunt side of the knife...
6.   ...and disarms A using the right forearm.

1. A strikes using Angle No. 1 (inwards from the outside at the neck).

2. D carries out a left-handed edge of the hand block outwards, while at the same time delivering a right-handed finger jab (disrupting technique) at the eyes and taking a lunging step 45° forwards to the right.

3. D places the right forearm on top of A's right forearm...

4. ...sweeps the weapon-bearing arm counter-clockwise downwards and outwards with the right hand...

5. ...grabs hold of the ball of A's right thumb with his left hand ...

6. ...places the edge of the right hand on the flat, blunt side of the knife...

7. ...and disarms A using the edge of the hand.

18.4 Angle No. 2 (Knife strike downwards and outwards from the inside at the neck)

1. A strikes using Angle No. 2 (from the inside at the neck).
2. D counters with an edge of the hand block upwards and outwards to the right, while at the same time delivering a left-handed finger jab (disrupting technique) at the head and taking a lunging step 45° forwards to the left.
3. With the right hand, D grabs hold of the ball of the thumb and leads A's arm clockwise downwards until the knife points at the ground.
4. D places the left hand (with the palm of the hand facing upwards) directly underneath A's right hand...
5. ...and disarms A using the left hand.

1. A strikes using Angle No. 2 (from the inside at the neck).

2. D counters with a block outwards using the edge of the right hand, while at the same time delivering a left-handed finger jab (disrupting action) at the eyes and taking a lunging step 45° forwards to the left.

3. With the right hand, D grabs hold of the ball of the thumb and leads the arm clockwise outwards to the left.

4. D stretches out his left arm (as if to tickle A). D places the flat, blunt side of the knife on top of the left upper arm.

5. With the right hand, D pulls A's right hand over the upper arm and disarms A using his own body.

1. A strikes using Angle No. 2 (from the inside at the neck).

2. D counters with a block outwards using the edge of the right hand, while at the same time delivering a left-handed finger jab (disrupting action) at the eyes and taking a lunging step 45° forwards to the left.

3. With the right hand, D grabs hold of the ball of the thumb...

4. ...and leads the arm clockwise behind the right side of A's back. In this movement a cut at liver height can be executed.

5. D places the blade on A's back...

6. ...and, with his right hand, he pulls A's right hand along close to his body and disarms A using the body.

18.5 Angle No. 3 (Knife strike from the outside at waist level)

1. A strikes using Angle No. 3 (from the outside at waist level).
2. D counters with a block downwards and outwards using the edge of the left hand, while at the same time delivering a right-handed finger jab (disrupting action) at the head and taking a lunging step 45° forwards to the right.
3. D places the right forearm on top of A's right forearm and sweeps the weapon-bearing arm counter-clockwise downwards and outwards to the right with his right hand. D takes a step backwards with the left leg as he does this, then he ...
4. ...grabs hold of the ball of the thumb with his left hand ...
5. ...places the right hand directly on top of A's right hand...
6. ...and disarms A using the right hand.

1. A strikes using Angle No. 3 (from the outside at waist level).

2. D counters with a block downwards and outwards using the edge of the left hand, while at the same time delivering a right-handed finger jab (disrupting action) at the head and taking a lunging step 45° forwards to the right.

3. D places the right forearm on top of A's right forearm...

4. ...sweeps the knife diagonally counter-clockwise downwards and outwards with his right hand, ...

5. ...grabs hold of the ball of A's right thumb with his left hand, and ...

6. ...places the right forearm on the flat, blunt side of the knife...

7. ...and disarms A using the right forearm.

1. A strikes using Angle No. 3 (from the outside at waist level).
2. D counters with a block downwards and outwards using the edge of the left hand, while at the same time delivering a right-handed finger jab (disrupting action) at the head and taking a lunging step 45° forwards to the right.
3. D places the right forearm on top of A's right forearm.
4. With the right hand, D sweeps the weapon-bearing arm counter-clockwise downwards to the right. As he does this, D takes a step backwards with the left leg...
5. ...and places his left hand underneath the right forearm...

6. ...while the right hand delivers another finger jab at the eyes (this action is called hammer and anvil).
7. With the right hand, D grabs hold of the ball of the thumb...
8. ...and leads the arm clockwise outwards to the left...
9. ...and then he stretches out the left arm and places the flat, blunt side of the knife on top of the left upper arm.
10. D pulls A's hand along over his upper arm with his right hand and disarms A over the left upper arm.

18.6 Angle No. 4 (Knife strike from the inside at waist level)

1. A strikes using Angle No. 4 (from the inside at waist level).
2. D counters with a block downwards and outwards using the edge of the right hand, while at the same time delivering a left-handed finger jab (disrupting action) at the eyes and taking a lunging step 45° forwards with the left foot to the left.

3. D places the left hand underneath the elbow...
4. ...and the right hand delivers another finger jab at the eyes.
5. With the right hand, D grabs hold of the ball of the thumb...
6. ...and pulls the arm clockwise downwards until the knife points at the ground.
7. D places the left hand directly underneath A's right hand and disarms A using the left hand (with the palm of the hand facing upwards).

1. A strikes using Angle No. 4 (from the inside at waist level).

2. D counters with a block downwards and outwards using the edge of the right hand, while at the same time delivering a left-handed finger jab (disrupting

action) at the eyes and taking a lunging step 45° forwards with the left foot to the left.

3. D places the left hand underneath the elbow...

4. ...and the right hand delivers another finger jab at the eyes.

5. With the right hand, D grabs hold of the ball of the thumb...

6. ...and pulls the arm clockwise outwards to the left.

7. D stretches out the left arm and places the flat, blunt side of the knife on top of the left upper arm.

8. With his right hand, D pulls A's right hand along over the upper arm and disarms A in this manner

1. A strikes using Angle No. 4 (from the inside at waist level).
2. D counters with a block downwards and outwards using the edge of the right hand,
   while at the same time delivering a left-handed finger jab (disrupting action) at the eyes and taking a lunging step 45° forwards with the left foot to the left.
3. With the right hand, D grabs hold of the ball of the thumb...
4. ...and leads the arm clockwise behind the right-hand side of A's back. In this movement a cut at liver height can be executed.
5. D places the blade on A's back...
6. ...and, with his right hand he pulls A's right hand along close to the body and disarms A over the body.

18.7 Angle No. 5 (Knife stab at the stomach)

1. A carries out a knife stab Angle No. 5 (at the stomach).

2. D counters with a block downwards and outwards using the edge of the right hand, while at the same time delivering a left-handed finger jab (disrupting action) at the head and taking a lunging step 45° forwards with the left foot to the left.

3. D places the left hand underneath A's elbow...

4. ...and the right hand delivers another finger jab at the eyes.

5. With the right hand, D grabs hold of the ball of the thumb...

6. ...and pulls the arm clockwise downwards until the knife points at the ground.

7. D carries out the disarming action with the left hand (with the palm of the hand facing upwards).

1. A carries out a knife stab Angle No. 5 (at the stomach).
2. D counters with a block downwards and outwards using the edge of the right hand, while at the same time delivering a left-handed finger jab (disrupting action) at   the head and taking a lunging step 45° forwards with the left foot to the left.
3. D places the left hand underneath A's right elbow...
4. ...and the right hand delivers another finger jab at the eyes.
5. With the right hand, D grabs hold of the ball of the thumb...
6. ...and leads the arm clockwise outwards to the left.
7. D stretches out the left arm and places the flat, blunt side of the knife on top of the left upper arm.
8. With his right hand, D pulls A's right hand along over the upper arm and disarms A over the left upper arm.

1. A carries out a knife stab Angle No. 5 (at the stomach).
2. D counters with a block downwards and outwards using the edge of the right hand, while at the same time delivering a left-handed finger jab (disrupting action) at the eyes and taking a lunging step 45° forwards with the left foot to the left.
3. D places the left hand underneath the right elbow...
4. ...and the right hand delivers another finger jab at the eyes.
5. With the right hand, D grabs hold of the ball of the thumb...
6. ...and leads the arm clockwise behind the right hand side of A's back. In this movement a cut at liver height can be executed.
7. D places the blade on A's back...
8. ...and with his right hand, D pulls A's right hand along over the upper arm and disarms A over the body.

19 Defense against Knife Attacks with Unarmed Follow-on Techniques

To a large extent, the first combination is the same for every attack angle. This has been done on purpose to show that you need only use one sequence of movements for all five attack angles.

19.1 Angle No. 1 (Knife strike downwards and inwards from the outside at the neck)

1. A strikes using Angle No. 1 (inwards from the outside at the neck).
2. D carries out a block upwards and outwards to the left with the edge of the hand while at the same time delivering a finger jab (disrupting action) to the right at the head and taking a lunging step 45° forwards to the right.
3. D places the right forearm underneath A's right arm...
4. ...leads the weapon-bearing arm with his right hand clockwise downwards to the right...
5. ...until the knife points at the ground and, at the same time, takes a step backwards with the right leg.

6. With the right hand, D grabs hold of the ball of A's thumb and carries out the disarming action with the left hand (with the palm of the left hand facing upwards).

7. D takes a step backwards with the right leg at an angle of at least 90° to A, and carries out a left-legged shinbone kick at the outside of A's right thigh.

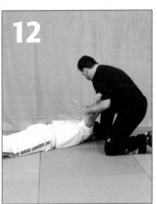

8. D brings his left arm clockwise from above...

9. ...round A's right arm...

10. ...and applies a twisting arm lock.

11. With the right hand, D presses A's head forwards and downwards at an angle of about 45° so that A cannot attack D's legs. D carries out a right-legged knee kick at A's head.

12. In this position, D forces A down to the ground and immobilizes him.

1. A strikes using Angle No. 1 (inwards from the outside at the neck).

2. D places his right forearm on top of A's right forearm, while at the same time delivering a left-handed finger jab (disrupting action) at A's eyes...

3. ...leads the weapon-bearing arm diagonal downwards and outwards with his right hand ...

4. ...grabbing hold of the ball of A's right thumb with his left hand...

5. ...and placing the right forearm on the flat, blunt side of the knife...

6. ...disarming A with the right forearm.

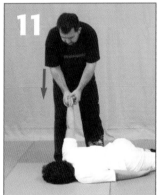

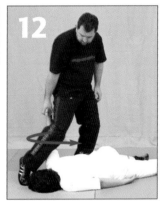

7. D leads his right arm clockwise under A's right arm...
8. ...and grabs A's elbow joint with his right hand coming in from the outside...
9. ...pulling the bent right arm counter-clockwise upwards to the right and forcing A down to the ground using the bent arm lock. D grabs A's right elbow from the outside...

10. ...and pulls A's right hand with his left hand , while at the same time applying pressure with his right hand against A's elbow...
11. ...and turns him over onto his stomach.
12. D places his right leg over A's outstretched right arm...
13. ...and immobilzes him on the ground by wrapping A's right arm round his right leg and kneeling on A's back with his right knee, applying a crossed-over grip with the leg.

1. A strikes using Angle No. 1 (inwards from the outside at the neck).

2. D carries out a block outwards with the edge of the left hand, while at the same time delivering a finger jab with the right hand (disrupting technique) at the eyes and taking a lunging step 45° forwards to the right.

3. He places the right forearm on top of A's right forearm...

4. ...and sweeps the weapon-bearing arm with his right hand counter-clockwise downwards and outwards...

5. ...grabbing hold of the ball of A's right thumb with his left hand.

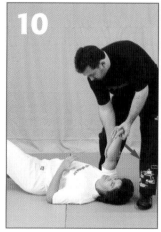

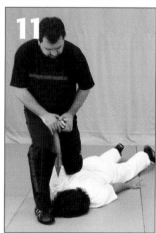

6. He then places the edge of the right hand on the flat, blunt side of the knife...

7. ...and carries out the disarming action with the edge of the hand.

8. D places his right hand on the back of A's right hand...

9. ...takes a step turn 90° backwards...

10. ...and throws A with a bent hand lock down to the ground. D grabs A's right elbow from the outside and pulls A's right hand with his left hand, while at the same time applying pressure with the right hand against A's elbow...

11. ...and turns A over onto his stomach. D places his left knee between A's shoulder blades and immobilizes him with a twisting hand lock. When doing this, D pushes his hips forward so that A is not able to pull his arm out (even without the hand being held).

19.2 Angle No. 2 (Knife strike downwards and outwards from the inside at the neck)

1. A strikes using Angle No. 2 (from the inside at the neck).
2. D counters with a block upwards and outwards to the right using the edge of the hand, while at the same time delivering a left-handed finger jab (disrupting action) at the head and taking a lunging step 45° forwards to the left.
3. With the right hand, D grabs hold of the ball of the thumb and leads A's arm clockwise downwards until the knife points at the ground.
4. He takes the knife out of the hand using his left hand (the palm of the hand is facing upwards).
5. D takes a step backwards with the right leg at an angle of at least 90° to A, and carries out a left-legged shinbone kick at the outside of A's right thigh.

6. D leads his left arm clockwise over A's right arm...

7. ...and further around A's right arm...

8. ...applying a twisting arm lock. With the right hand, D presses A's head forwards and downwards at an angle of about 45° so that A cannot attack D's legs.

9. D carries out a right-legged knee kick at A's head.

10. In this position, D forces A down to the ground, immobilizing him.

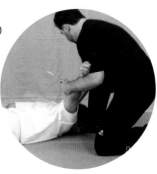

1. A strikes using Angle No. 2 (from the inside at the neck).
2. D counters with a block outwards using the edge of the right hand, while at the same time delivering a left-handed finger jab (disrupting action) at the eyes and taking a lunging step 45° forwards to the left.
3. With the right hand, D grabs hold of the ball of the thumb and leads the arm clockwise outwards to the left.
4. D stretches out his left arm (as if to tickle A). D places the flat, blunt side of the knife on top of the left upper arm.
5. ...and with his right hand, D pulls A's right hand along over the upper arm and disarms A over the body.

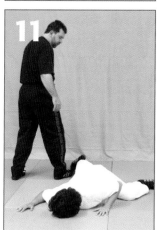

6.   D carries out a left-handed palm heel strike at A's genitalia...

7.   ...and then brings A's right arm outwards with the left arm...

8.   ...securing A's right arm with the left hand, carrying out another palm heel strike with the right hand at A's genitalia...

9.   He then places his right leg in front of A's right leg and pulls A's right arm inwards (taking the weight off A's right leg).

10. D sweeps the right leg at an angle of 45° backwards...

11. ...so that A is forced to fall down forwards.

1.   A strikes using Angle No. 2 (from the inside at the neck).

2. D counters with a block outwards using the edge of the right hand, while at the same time delivering a left-handed finger jab (disrupting action) at the eyes and taking a lunging step 45° forwards to the left.

3. With the right hand, D grabs hold of the ball of the thumb...

4. ...and leads the arm clockwise behind the right hand side of A's back. In this movement a cut at liver height can be executed.

5. D places the blade on A's back and pulls A's right hand along close to the body with his right hand...

6. ...carrying out the disarming action over the body.

7. D grabs hold of A's neck with his left hand...

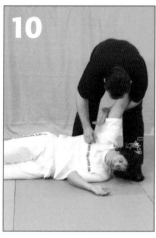

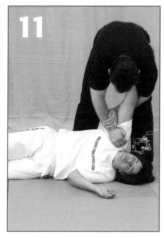

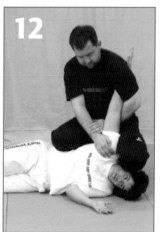

8. ...and places his right hand in A's face...

9. ...forcing A down to the ground using a twisting neck hold.

10. D leads his left arm round A's right arm...

11. ...places the right hand on A's right shoulder, while the left hand grasps hold of his own right wrist.

12. D kneels down with his left knee on A's head and the right knee on the right hand side of A's upper body. D ends the combination with a stretched arm lock (inside arm lock).

105

19.3 Angle No. 3 (Knife strike from the outside at waist level)

1. A strikes using Angle No. 3 (from the outside at waist level).

2. D counters using a block with the edge of the hand downwards and outwards to the left, while at the same time delivering a right-handed finger jab (disrupting action) at the head and taking a lunging step 45° forwards to the right.

3. With the right hand, D sweeps the weapon-bearing arm counter-clockwise downwards to the right. At the same time D takes a step backwards with the left leg...

4. ...grabs hold of the ball of the thumb with his left hand ...

5. ...places the right hand directly on top of A's right hand...

6. ...and takes the weapon out of A's hand with his right hand.

7. D takes a step backwards with the right leg at an angle of at least 90° to A...

8. ...and carries out a left-legged shinbone kick at the outside of A's right thigh.

9. D leads his left arm clockwise from above over A's right arm...

10. ...and applies a twisting arm lock. With the right hand, D presses A's head forwards and downwards at an angle of about 45° so that A cannot attack D's legs.

11. In this position, D forces A down to the ground and immobilizes him.

1. A strikes using Angle No. 3 (from the outside at waist level).
2. D counters using a block with the edge of the hand downwards and outwards to the left, while at the same time delivering a right-handed finger jab (disrupting action) at the head and taking a lunging step 45° forwards to the right.
3. D places the right forearm on top of A's right forearm...
4. ...and sweeps the knife counter-clockwise diagonally downwards and outwards ...

5. ...grabbing hold of the ball of A's right thumb with his left hand and twists A's right wrist clockwise so that the knife is pointing outwards to the left...

6. ...then places the right forearm on the flat, blunt side of the knife...

7. ...and disarms A with the forearm.

8. D rolls the right arm over A's right arm...

9. ...places the right hand on A's chest moving behind him as he does this and carries out a left-handed stranglehold.

1. A strikes using Angle No. 3 (from the outside at waist level).
2. D counters using a block with the edge of the hand downwards and outwards to the left, while at the same time delivering a right-handed finger jab (disrupting action) at the head and taking a lunging step 45° forwards to the right.
3. D places the right forearm on top of A's right forearm...
4. ...and brings the weapon-bearing arm counter-clockwise downwards to the right. At the same time D takes a step backwards with the left leg.
5. D places his left hand underneath the right forearm...
6. ...and the right hand delivers another finger jab at the eyes (this position is called hammer and anvil).

7. With the right hand, D grabs hold of the ball of the thumb...

8. ...and leads the arm clockwise outwards to the left...

9. ...stretches out the left arm and places the flat, blunt side of the knife on top of the left forearm...

10. ...and pulls A's right hand along over the forearm with his right hand and disarms A.

11. D places the left hand on A's right elbow...

12. ...and applies a stretched arm lock to bring him down to the ground.

19.4 Angle No. 4 (Knife strike from the inside at waist level)

1. A strikes using Angle No. 4 (from the inside at waist level).
2. D counters using a block with the edge of the right hand downwards and outwards, while at the same time delivering a left-handed finger jab (disrupting action) at the head and taking a lunging step 45° forwards to the left.
3. D places the left hand underneath the elbow...
4. ...and the right hand delivers another finger jab at the eyes.
5. With the right hand, D grabs hold of the ball of the thumb and pulls the arm clockwise downwards until the knife points at the ground.

6. D places the left hand directly underneath A's right hand...

7. ...and takes the knife out of A's hand with his left hand (the palm of the hand is facing upwards).

8. D takes a step backwards with the right leg at an angle of at least 90° to A... and carries out a left-legged shinbone kick at the outside of A's right thigh.

9. D leads his left arm clockwise from above around A's right arm...

10. ...and applies a twisting arm lock. With the right hand, D presses A's head forwards and downwards at an angle of about 45° so that A cannot attack D's legs.

11. In this position, D forces A down to the ground, immobilizing him.

1. A strikes using Angle No. 4 (from the inside at waist level).
2. D counters using a block with the edge of the hand downwards and outwards to the left, while at the same time delivering a right-handed finger jab (disrupting action) at the head and taking a lunging step 45° forwards to the right.
3. D places the left hand underneath the elbow...
4. ...and the right hand delivers another finger jab at the eyes.
5. With the right hand, D grabs hold of the ball of the thumb and pulls the arm clockwise downwards to the left.

114

6. D places the edge of the left hand on the flat, blunt side of the knife...

7. ...and disarms A with the edge of the hand.

8. D leads his left arm over A's right arm...

9. ...coils it round his left arm...

10. ...and grabs hold of A's bent right hand applying a coiled arm lock with his left hand.

11. D places the fore and middle finger of his right hand in the hollow under A's right ear and applies pressure on the nerve.

1. A strikes using Angle No. 4 (from the inside at waist level).
2. D counters using a block with the edge of the right hand downwards and outwards, while at the same time delivering a left-handed finger jab (disrupting action) at the head and taking a lunging step 45° forwards to the left.
3. D grabs hold of the ball of A's right thumb with his left hand...
4. ...and places the right forearm on the flat, blunt side of the knife.
5. D levers the knife out of A's hand with the right forearm...

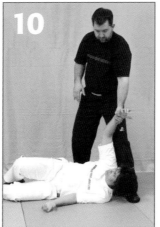

6.   ...and brings his right hand past the right hand side of A's head onto his neck...

7.   ...lifts A's left hand up with his left hand...

8.   ...and with his right hand D brings A's head onto D's left elbow...

9.   ...moves round behind A and then pulls the right hand and presses the head downwards...

10. ...and brings A down to the ground with a twist throw...

11. ...ending the combination with a low kick at A's head.

19.5 Angle No. 5 (Knife stab at the stomach)

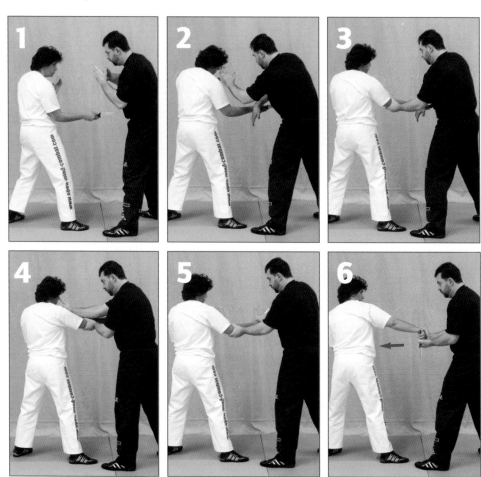

1. A stabs using Angle No. 5 (at the stomach).
2. D counters using a block with the edge of the right hand downwards and outwards to the right, while at the same time delivering a left-handed finger jab (disrupting action) at the head and taking a lunging step 45° forwards to the left.
3. D places the left hand underneath A's right elbow...
4. ...and the right hand delivers another finger jab at the eyes.
5. D keeps hold of A's elbow and with the right hand, D grabs hold of the ball of the thumb...
6. ...and pulls the arm clockwise downwards until the knife points at the ground...

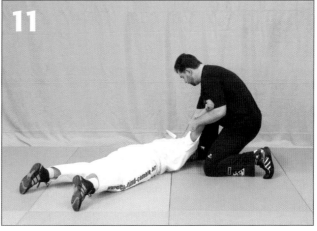

7. ...and takes the knife out of A's hand with his left hand (the palm of the hand is facing upwards).

8. D takes a step backwards with the right leg at an angle of at least 90° to A and carries out a left-legged shinbone kick at the outside of A's right thigh.

9. D leads his left arm clockwise from above around A's right arm...

10. ...and applies a twisting arm lock. With the right hand, D presses A's head forwards and downwards at an angle of about 45° so that A cannot attack D's legs.

11. In this position, D forces A down to the ground, immobilizing him.

1. A stabs using Angle No. 5 (at the stomach).
2. D counters using a block with the edge of the right hand downwards and outwards to the right, while at the same time delivering a left-handed finger jab (disrupting action) at the head and taking a lunging step 45° forwards to the left.
3. D places the left hand underneath A's right elbow...
4. ...and the right hand delivers another finger jab at the eyes.
5. With the right hand, D grabs hold of the ball of the thumb...
6. ...and carries out an armbreaker to A's right elbow with his outstretched arm. A is then disarmed.

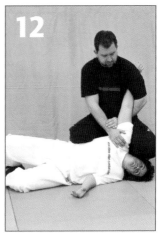

7. With the left arm, D leads A's right arm counter-clockwise upwards and outwards...

8. ...grabs hold of A's chin with the right hand...

9. ...places the left hand in the area of A's loin (lower back)...

10. ...and forces A to the ground by bending his body over.

11. D leads his left arm round A's right arm...

12. ...kneels down with his left knee on A's neck and the right knee on the right side of A's upper body and ends the combination with an inside arm lock (stretching arm lock).

1. A stabs using Angle No. 5 (at the stomach).
2. D counters with a right-handed sweeping block counter-clockwise downwards and outwards to the right, while at the same time delivering a left-handed finger jab at A's eyes...
3. ...brings the weapon-bearing hand further upwards towards A's head with his right hand ...
4. ...places the flat, blunt side of the knife on A's neck...

5. ...and pulls the weapon-bearing hand forwards (with the flat, blunt side of the knife) along close to the neck. At the same time, D presses A's head backwards (counter-pressure) with his left hand and disarms A over his neck.

6. With the left hand, D grabs hold of A's right wrist...

7. ...places the right hand on the back of A's right hand and applies a bent hand lock.

8. D forces A to the ground using a bent hand lock.

20 Defense against Knife Attacks - Disarming and using the weapon to control the opponent

In this section, I put the main focus on controlling the attacker after disarming the knife and not to go on to hurt him by using strikes or stabs.

To a large extent, the first combination is the same for every attack angle. This has been done on purpose to show that you need only use one sequence of movements for all five attack angles.

20.1 Angle No. 1 (Knife strike downwards and inwards from the outside at the neck)

1. A strikes using Angle No. 1 (inwards from the outside at the neck).
2. D counters using a block with the edge of the hand upwards and outwards to the left, while at the same time delivering a right-handed finger jab (disrupting action) at the head and taking a lunging step 45° forwards to the right.
3. D places the right hand underneath A's right arm...

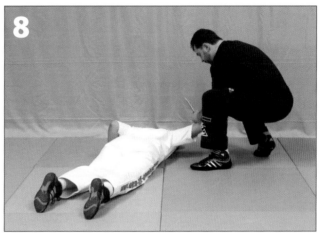

4.   ...brings the weapon-bearing arm clockwise downwards to the right with his right hand ...

5.   ...until the knife points at the ground and takes a step backwards with the right leg and then D grabs hold of the ball of A's thumb with his right hand, ...

6.   ...and carries out the disarming action with the left hand (the palm of the left hand is facing upwards).

7.   D places the blade on top of A's right elbow and pulls A's right arm with his right hand.

8.   D applies a stretched arm lock to bring A down to the ground.

1. A strikes using Angle No. 1 (inwards from the outside at the neck).
2. With his right hand, D brings the weapon-bearing arm diagonally counter-clockwise inwards, while at the same time delivering a left-handed finger jab (disrupting action) at A's eyes.
3. With the left hand, D grabs hold of the ball of A's right thumb...
4. ...places the right hand closely on top of A's right hand...
5. ...and disarms A with the hand.
6. D leads the weapon-bearing hand further forwards and places the knife handle on top of A's collarbone. When he does this, D is standing behind A. D now grabs hold of his own right hand with his left hand and applies strong pressure on A's collarbone with the knife handle.
7. As a result, A is forced down to the ground. With the right leg, D immobilizes A's right arm.

1. A strikes using Angle No. 1 (inwards from the outside at the neck).

2. D counters using a block with the edge of the left hand outwards, while at the same time delivering a left-handed finger jab (disrupting action) at the head and taking a lunging step 45° forwards to the right.

3. With his right hand, D sweeps the weapon-bearing arm counter-clockwise downwards and outwards ...

4. ...grabs hold of the ball of A's right thumb with his left hand ...

5. ...turns A's right wrist so that the knife is pointing outwards to the left.

6. D places his right hand closely on top of A's right hand and disarms A with the hand.

7. D brings his right arm round A's right arm and carries out a bent arm lock. D places the knife handle on top of A's right collarbone and then grabs hold of his own right hand with his left hand and applies strong pressure on A's collarbone with the knife handle.

8. As a result, A is forced down to the ground.

20.2 Angle No. 2 (Knife strike downwards and outwards from the inside at the neck)

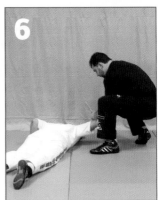

1. A strikes using Angle No. 2 (from the inside at the neck).
2. D counters using a block with the edge of the hand upwards and outwards to the right, while at the same time delivering a left-handed finger jab (disrupting action) at the head and taking a lunging step 45° forwards to the left.
3. With the right hand, D grabs hold of the ball of the thumb and leads A's arm clockwise downwards until the knife points at the ground.
4. With his left hand D takes the knife out of the hand (the palm of the hand is facing upwards).
5. D places the blade on top of A's right elbow and pulls A's right arm with his right hand.
6. D applies a stretched arm lock to bring A down to the ground.

1. A strikes using Angle No. 2 (from the inside at the neck).

2. D counters using a block with the edge of the right hand outwards, while at the same time delivering a left-handed finger jab (disrupting action) at the eyes and taking a lunging step 45° forwards to the left.

3. With the right hand, D grabs hold of the ball of the thumb and leads the arm clockwise outwards to the left until the knife points at the ground.

4. D places the left hand on the flat, blunt side of the knife. The palm of the hand is facing upwards and D's and A's forefingers touch each other. D disarms A with the hand...

5. ...leads his left arm clockwise round A's right arm...

6. ...applying a twisting arm lock (stretched arm lock) and presses A's head at an angle of about 45° forwards and downwards towards the ground with his right hand.

7. With the twisting arm lock, D forces A down to the ground and immobilizes him.

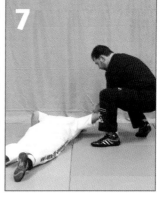

1. A strikes using Angle No. 2 (from the inside at the neck).

2. D counters using a block with the edge of the right hand outwards, while at the same time delivering a left-handed finger jab (disrupting action) at the eyes and taking a lunging step 45° forwards to the left.

3. With the right hand, D grabs hold of the ball of the thumb and leads the arm clockwise behind the right hand side of A's back. In this movement a cut at liver height can be executed.

4. D places the blade on A's back and pulls A's right hand along close to his body with his right hand...

5. ...and disarms A over the body. While A loses his grip on the knife, D takes hold of the knife handle with his left hand.

6. D brings his left arm around A's neck from behind and places the knife blade on the right side of A's neck and brings A's right arm up behind A's back in a bent arm lock. In this position, A can be moved about ('transporting lever').

20.3 Angle No. 3 (Knife strike from the outside at waist level)

1. A strikes using Angle No. 3 (from the outside at waist level).
2. D counters using a block with the edge of the hand downwards and outwards to the left, while at the same time delivering a right-handed finger jab (disrupting action) at the head and taking a lunging step 45° forwards to the right.
3. D places the right forearm on top of A's right forearm...
4. ...brings the weapon-bearing arm counter-clockwise downwards to the right with his right hand. As he does this D takes a step backwards with the left leg...

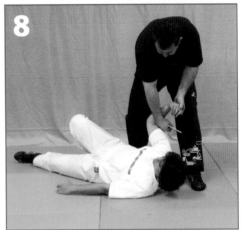

5. ...grabs hold of the ball of the thumb with the left hand...

6. ...and takes the knife out of A's hand with his right hand.

7. D places the blade on A's right elbow joint...

8. ...pulls A's arm counter-clockwise upwards and brings A down to the ground using a bent arm lock.

1. A strikes using Angle No. 3 (from the outside at waist level).
2. With the right hand, D sweeps the knife diagonally counter-clockwise downwards and outwards, while at the same time delivering a left-handed finger jab (disrupting action) at the eyes and turning to the left.
3. With the left hand, D grabs hold of the ball of A's right thumb...
4. ...places the right hand on the flat, blunt side of the knife so that both forefingers touch each other...

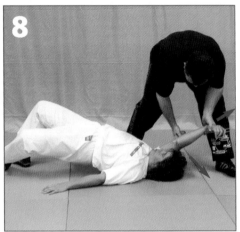

5. …and takes the knife off A with the right hand.

6. D places the knife handle a little below the knuckle of the ring finger, takes a step turning 90° to the rear…

7. …and throws A down to the ground with a bent hand lock.

8. D places the blade on A's right elbow and pulls the right arm with his left hand at. D immobilizes A using a stretched arm lock on the ground.

1. A strikes using Angle No. 3 (from the outside at waist level).
2. D counters using a block with the edge of the hand downwards and outwards to the left, while at the same time delivering a right-handed finger jab (disrupting action) at the head and taking a lunging step 45° forwards to the right.
3. D places the right forearm on top of A's right forearm...
4. ...and brings the weapon-bearing arm counter-clockwise downwards to the right with his right hand.
   As he does this D takes a step backwards with the left leg.
5. D places his left hand underneath the right forearm...

135

6. ...and the right hand delivers another finger jab at the eyes (hammer and anvil).

7. With the right hand, D grabs hold of the ball of the thumb...

8. ...leads the arm clockwise outwards to the left until the knife points at the ground. D places the left hand (the palm of the hand is facing upwards) on the flat, blunt side of the knife...

9. ...and disarms A with the hand.

10. D places the knife handle on A's elbow joint and pulls it to the left. D immobilizes A using a twisting hand lock (in the form of a Z-shaped lever).

20.4 Angle No. 4 (Knife strike from the inside at waist level)

1. A strikes using Angle No. 4 (from the inside at waist level).
2. D counters using a block with the edge of the right hand downwards and outwards, while at the same time delivering a left-handed finger jab (disrupting action) at the eyes and taking a lunging step 45° forwards to the left.
3. D places the left hand underneath the elbow...
4. ...and the right hand delivers another finger jab at the eyes.

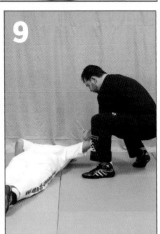

5. With the right hand, D grabs hold of the ball of the thumb...

6. ...and pulls the arm clockwise downwards until the knife points at the ground.

7. D takes the knife out of A's hand with his left hand (the palm of the hand is facing upwards).

8. D places the blade on top of A's right elbow and pulls A's right arm with his right hand...

9. ...bringing A down to the ground applying a stretched arm lock.

1. A strikes using Angle No. 4 (from the inside at waist level).
2. D counters using a block with the edge of the right hand downwards and outwards, while at the same time delivering a left-handed finger jab (disrupting action) at the eyes and taking a lunging step 45° forwards to the left.
3. With the left hand, D grabs hold of the ball of A's right thumb...
4. ...places his right hand on top of A's right hand so that both forefingers touch each other...
5. 1...and carries out the disarming action forwards with the hand.
6. D places the knife handle on the back of A's right hand...
7. ...and brings A down to the ground using a bent hand lock.

1. A strikes using Angle No. 4 (from the inside at waist level).
2. D counters using a block with the edge of the right hand downwards and outwards, while at the same time delivering a left-handed finger jab (disrupting action) at the eyes and taking a lunging step 45° forwards to the left.
3. With the left hand, D grabs hold of the ball of A's right thumb.
4. D turns A's right hand counter-clockwise until the knife points to the left. D places the right thumb on the knife handle...

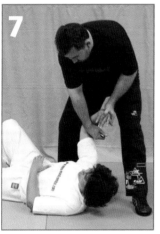

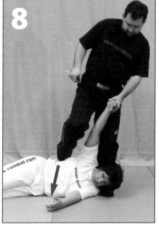

5. ...and levers the knife out of A's hand. D now holds the knife in the dagger position (the blade is on the side of the little finger).

6. D places the blade on the outside of A's right elbow and angles his right arm. With the knife D pulls the angled arm inwards...

7. ...and brings A down to the ground using a bent arm lock.

8. D carries out a right-footed kick on A's lower ribcage (right-hand side of the upper body) so that A can be turned onto his stomach easily...

9. ...and finally immobilizes him with a stretched arm lock over the groin.

20.5   Angle No. 5 (Knife stab at the stomach)

1.   A stabs using Angle No. 5 (at the stomach).
2.   D counters using a block with the edge of the hand downwards and outwards to the right, while at the same time delivering a left-handed finger jab (disrupting action) at the head and taking a lunging step 45° forwards to the left.
3.   D places the left hand underneath A's right elbow...
4.   ...and the right hand delivers another finger jab at the eyes.

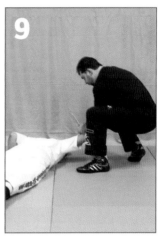

5. With the right hand, D grabs hold of the ball of the thumb...

6. ...and pulls the arm clockwise downwards until the knife points at the ground.

7. D takes the knife out of A's hand with the left hand (the palm of the hand is facing upwards).

8. D places the blade on top of A's right elbow and pulls A's right arm with his right hand.

9. D applies a stretched arm lock to bring A down to the ground.

1. A stabs using Angle No. 5 (at the stomach).
2. D counters using a block with the edge of the hand downwards and outwards to the right, while at the same time delivering a left-handed finger jab (disrupting action) at the head and taking a lunging step 45° forwards to the left.
3. D places the left hand underneath A's right elbow...
4. ...and the right hand delivers another finger jab at the eyes.

5. With the right hand, D grabs hold of the ball of A's right thumb.

6. With the left arm, D reaches clockwise over A's right arm...

7. ...coils A's right arm round his left arm...

8. ...grabs hold of A's bent right hand with his left hand, applying a coiled arm lock. D disarms A with the right hand...

9. ...and places the knife underneath A's right ear. With this combination, A can be moved about ('transporting lever').

1. A stabs using Angle No. 5 (at the stomach).

2. D counters with a right-handed sweeping block counter-clockwise downwards and outwards to the right, while at the same time delivering a left-handed finger jab at A's eyes.

3. With the left hand, D grabs hold of the ball of A's right thumb...

4. ...and twists the hand counter-clockwise until the knife points to the left. D places his right thumb on the end of the knife handle...

5. ...and levers the knife out of A's hand. D now holds the knife in the dagger position (with the blade on the side of the little finger).

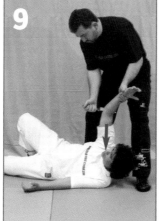

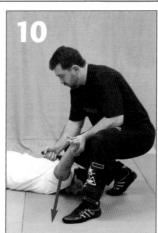

6. D brings his right hand onto the right hand side of A's neck...

7. ...and wedges A's neck between the blade and the right forearm. D presses A's left arm upwards...

8. ...and at the same time he brings A's head clockwise downwards and inwards...

9. ...and brings A down to the ground using a twisting throw. D places the blade on the outside of A's right elbow...

10. ...pulling A's right arm and turning him onto his stomach. D immobilizes A on the ground using a stretched arm lock.

20.6   Exercise

Defense against Knife Attack Angles No. 1-5 combined with disrupting techniques; controlling the weapon-bearing arm; disarming and follow-on techniques (exercising with a partner).

Sequence
A attacks D using Knife Attack Angles No. 1-5. D applies what he has learned i. e. he uses disrupting techniques; tries to control the weapon-bearing arm; disarms A; and applies follow-on techniques. The exercises should take place in a form of sparring where A does not reply with his full effort.

21 Free Self-defense against Announced Multiple Knife Attacks

21.1 Attack Combination 1: Straight Punch and Knife Strike (Angle No. 1)

1. A delivers a left-handed punch at D's head.
2. With the right hand, D sweeps the left arm inwards...
3. ...circles the right hand round A's left hand (Scoop)...
4. ...and carries out a hand jab at A's larynx.
5. A strikes using Angle No. 1 (from the outside at D's, neck).
6. D places the right forearm on top of A's forearm...
7. ...and brings the weapon-bearing arm diagonally with the right forearm outwards...

8. ...delivers a left-handed finger jab at the eyes...
9. ...grabs hold of the ball of A's right thumb with the left hand...
10. ...places the right forearm on the flat, blunt side of the knife...
11. ...and disarms A with the right forearm.
12. With the own right arm, D reaches counter-clockwise over A's right arm...
13. ...presses A's right arm further backwards...
14. ...places the right hand on A's chest and carries out a bent arm lock, grabbing hold of A's larynx with the left hand.

21.2 Attack Combination 2: Knife Strike (Angle No. 2) and Straight Punch at the Head

1. A strikes using Angle No. 2 (from the inside at D's neck).
2. D executes a block outwards to the right using the edge of the right hand, while at the same time delivering a finger jab at A's eyes.
3. With the right hand, D grabs hold of the ball of A's right thumb...
4. ...and brings the weapon-bearing arm clockwise outwards to the left (past his own body)...
5. ...stretches out his left arm (underneath A's right arm)...
6. ...and disarms A over the left upper arm.
7. A delivers a left-handed punch at D's head.

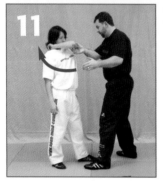

8. With the right hand, D sweeps A's left arm clockwise inwards and simultaneously in the same movement he strikes A's eyes...

9. ...bringing the arm clockwise outwards further...

10. ...and then continues clockwise downwards...

11. ...bringing the arm further clockwise upwards at A's head.

12. D leads his own left arm past A's left arm (which is in front of A's neck)...

13. ...places the right fist in the region of A's left kidney...

14. ...and brings A down to the ground.

21.3 Attack Combination 3: Knife Stab No. 5 (at the Stomach) and Shinbone Kick

1. A delivers a knife stab Angle No. 5 at D's stomach.
2. With his right forearm, D carries out a block downwards and outwards.
3. A delivers a right-legged shinbone kick at the outside of D's left thigh. D brings his left leg up high and directs the left kneecap towards A's attacking right-legged shinbone (this is very painful for A).
4. With the left hand, D grabs hold of the ball of A's right thumb...

5. ...and twists the weapon-bearing hand counter-clockwise outwards to the left. D places the right thumb on the knife handle...

6. ...and disarms A with the hand (now, D holds the knife in the dagger position).

7. D bends A's right arm and places the blade on the outside of A's right upper arm near the elbow. D pulls the arm inwards...

8. ...and brings A down to the ground using a bent arm lock.

21.4 Attack Combination 4: Knife Strikes No. 1 and No. 3

1. A strikes using Angle No. 1 (from the outside at D's neck).
2. D carries out a block using the edge of the left hand upwards and outwards to the left.
3. A pulls back the knife and strikes using Angle No. 3 (from the outside at D's stomach).
4. D places the right forearm on top of A's right forearm...
5. ...carries out a right-handed sweeping action counter-clockwise downwards and outwards to the right...

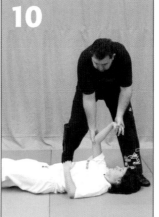

6. ...grabs hold of the ball of A's right thumb with his left hand ...

7. ...places the right forearm on the flat, blunt side of the knife...

8. ...and disarms A with the right forearm.

9. D brings his right arm clockwise under A's right arm and grabs A's elbow joint from the outside with the fingers. D pulls A's right arm upwards...

10. ...and brings A down to the ground using the bent arm lock.

11. A circular foot kick at A's head ends the combination.

21.5 Attack Combination 5: Knife Strike No. 2 and Knife Stab No. 5

1. A strikes using Angle No. 2 (from the inside at D's neck).
2. D carries out a block using the edge of the right hand upwards and outwards to the right.
3. ...and places the left hand underneath A's right elbow.
4. With the right leg, A takes a step backwards, at the same time pulling the weapon back.
5. With the right leg, A takes a step forwards and stabs using Angle No. 5 (at D's stomach).
6. With the right hand, D sweeps the weapon-bearing arm counter-clockwise downwards and outwards to the right...
7. ...places the left hand underneath A's right elbow...

8. ...carries out a right-handed finger jab at A's eyes...

9. ...grabs hold of the ball of A's right thumb with his right hand...

10. ...and brings the weapon-bearing arm clockwise downwards and outwards to the left. D places the left forearm on the flat, blunt side of the knife...

11. ...and disarms A with the left forearm.

12. D pulls the weapon-bearing arm forwards...

13. ...grabs hold of A's left neck muscle with his left hand from behind and turns A round (so that A has his back to D).
14. D brings his right arm round A's neck...
15. ...lays his right hand on top of his left shoulder...
16. ...slides the left hand behind the back of A's head (with the back of the hand facing the back of A's head)...
17. ...pulls his own shoulder blades together and applies a stranglehold technique (Mata Leao) using the arms.

22 Self-defense against a Knife Threat in the Grappling range

22.1 The Blade of the Knife is in Contact with the Body

1. A is standing in front of D with his left hand on D's neck, and holds the knife at D's stomach.
2. With both hands, D grabs hold of A's weapon-bearing arm. For this, the left hand is above the weapon-bearing arm and the right hand is underneath it. Simultaneously, D takes a step turn 90° to the rear.

3. D twists A's right arm round so that the elbow is lying against D's left side of the upper body then turns to the right and levers A's right arm over his upper body...

4. ...so that A is forced to move forward...

5. ...places the right hand on the back of A's right hand and takes a step turn or double step turn.

6. D brings A down to the ground using a twisting hand lock and places the right thumb on the knife handle...

7. ...and disarms A...

8. ...ending the combination with a circular foot kick at A's head.

1. A is standing in front of D with his left hand on D's neck, and holds the knife at D's larynx with his right hand.

2. With both hands, D grabs hold of A's weapon-bearing arm. For this, the left hand is above the weapon-bearing arm and the right hand is underneath it. Simultaneously, D takes a step turn 90° to the rear.

3. D twists A's right arm round so that A's elbow is facing upwards.

4. D applies a body lock (stretched arm lock). D places A's right elbow directly underneath his left armpit. By pulling A's arm and pressing his armpit, D creates a leverage.

5.   With the left hand, D carries out a back-handed punch at A's head...

6.   ...bends A's right hand (a form of a bent hand lock)...

7.   ...and places the left hand on the flat, blunt side of the knife...

8.   ...and disarms A with the hand.

1. A stands on the right hand side behind D, holding the knife in his right hand (behind D's right arm) in the direction of D's kidney while grasping D's left arm from behind with his left hand.

2. D presses his bent right arm backwards against the flat, blunt side of the knife and presses it with his upper arm against A's upper body.

3. With his left hand, D grabs hold of A's right wrist...

4. ...carries out a head butt (disrupting action) at A's head...

5. ...and disarms A by pulling A's right arm forwards.

6. With his right forearm, D strikes at A's right elbow joint from underneath and in doing so carries out an armbreaker.

7. With both hands, D brings A's right arm clockwise inwards...

8. ...places his left forearm on top of A's right elbow...

9. ...and ends the combination with a stretched arm lock.

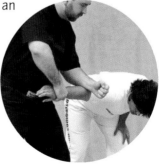

1. A stands on the right hand side behind D, holding the knife in his right hand (in front of D's right arm) in the direction of D's liver while grasping D's left arm from behind with his left hand.

2. D turns inwards, pulls his right arm outwards and in the same movement presses A's weapon-bearing wrist firmly at A's stomach with his left hand.

3. D carries out a head butt (disrupting action) at A's head...

4. ...and with his right forearm/upper arm pushes against the flat, blunt side of the knife towards and holds it against A's upper body.

5. D disarms A by pulling A's right arm forwards.

6. With his right forearm, D strikes at A's right elbow joint from underneath and in doing so carries out an armbreaker.

7. With both hands, D brings A's right arm clockwise inwards...

8. ...bringing A's right arm further round onto his back (bent arm lock) grabbing the hair with his right hand...

9. ...and places his right foot into the hollow of A's right knee.

1. A stands besides D with his left arm round D's neck, and presses the knife against the right side of D's neck with his right hand.

2. D turns his head away outwards and in the same movement he brings his right arm upwards...

3. ...carries out a punch with his elbow upwards and rearwards with the right arm...

4. ...grabbing hold of A's right weapon-bearing wrist with his right hand, and carrying out a left-handed punch with the ball of the hand at A's face...

5. ...bringing the weapon-bearing arm clockwise outwards to the left until the knife points at the ground, places his left hand on the handle of A's knife...

6. ...and disarms A with the hand.

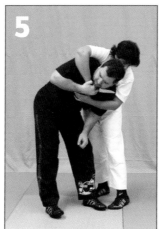

1. A is standing behind D with the knife in his right hand laid round D's left hand side of the neck. A's left arm is lying on D's chest.

2. With his right hand, D grabs hold of A's right weapon-bearing wrist and presses it hard against his own neck so that A cannot use the weapon for cutting. A would have to be able to pull the knife to the right in order to cut D. D must prevent this.

3. D brings his left arm forwards in order to create momentum...

4. ...and carries out a punch (hammer blow) at A's genitalia...

5. ...turns round inwards under A's right arm...

6. ...applying strong pressure on A's right elbow with his right shoulder and executes a stretched arm lock. In this position, D could disarm A using the left hand.

22.2 Against a Wall

22.2.1 D stands with his back to the wall

1. D stands with his back to the wall and A is in front of him. A strikes using Angle No. 1 (Knife strike downwards from the outside at the neck).
2. With the right hand, D sweeps/brings the weapon-bearing arm diagonally counter-clockwise downwards and outwards.
3. With the left hand, D grasps behind A's back and hooks his fingers onto the back of A's neck muscles.
4. D now turns A round A counter-clockwise and throws him against the wall. With his right hand, D continues to keep hold of A's weapon-bearing arm.
5. A's outstretched right arm lies against the wall.
6. With a punch with the ball of the hand, D demolishes A's right elbow joint and creates a disarming action.

7. D places his right foot next to A's left foot...

8. ...and carries out a sweep of the foot with his left leg against A's left leg.

1. D stands with his back to the wall and A is in front of him. A strikes using Angle No. 1 (knife strike downwards from the outside at the neck).

2. With the right hand, D sweeps/brings the weapon-bearing arm diagonally counter-clockwise downwards and outwards to the right...

3. ...and takes hold of the arm with his left hand behind A's elbow.

4. A brings the arm counter-clockwise (as seen by D) round in a circle further upwards...

5. ...and delivers a left-handed punch at D's head.

6. With the right hand, D sweeps the punch inwards and stands now besides (90°) A...

7. ...and then grasps through under his arm with the left hand, grabbing hold of the left wrist...

8. ...and pulling A's fist further forwards so that he strikes it against the wall.

9. After that, D pulls A's left fist downwards along the wall (so that the skin will be grazed). In case of another attack, depending on the chosen attack angle, one of the defense techniques already described can be used.

1. D stands with his back to the wall and A is in front of him. A strikes using Angle No. 1 (knife strike downwards from the outside at the neck).
2. D sweeps/brings the weapon-bearing arm further downwards and outwards...
3. ...takes hold of the weapon-bearing wrist with the right hand and brings it onto A's neck...
4. ...laying the flat, blunt side of the knife on the left side behind A's neck.
5. With the left hand, D presses frontally against A's head...
6. ...and then pulls A's right hand with his right hand and disarms A over his neck.
    Warning: If A does not loosen his grip of the knife or D doesn't take care that the flat, blunt side of the knife is lying on the neck, A is in danger of being severely injured. A cut on the neck could result in A's death.

1. A places the knife against D's chest.
2. With the left hand, D grabs hold of A's weapon-bearing hand, tilts the wrist (of the weapon-bearing hand) towards A, while delivering at the same time a right-handed stab at A's larynx.

3. D brings the knife over A's liver...
4. ...places the knife (with the flat, blunt side) in the region of A's kidneys...
5. ...pulls the hand along forwards close to A's body and disarms A over the body.
6. D brings his left arm clockwise round A's right arm, grabs hold of A's neck with the right hand...
7. ...takes a step turn 90° rearwards and pulls A's head towards the wall.
8. D brings A down to the ground with a twisting throw.

1. A strikes using Angle No. 2 from the inside at D's neck.
2. With the right hand, D grabs hold of A's weapon-bearing wrist and brings the left arm through under the weapon-bearing arm.
3. D places the left shoulder against A's right upper arm, levers the right arm over the left shoulder...
4. ...and shoves A against the wall. D immobilizes A against the wall...
5. ...pulls the outstretched arm further to the left...
6. ...until A loosens his hold on the knife.

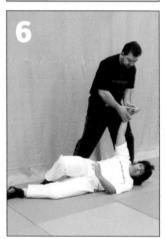

1. A strikes using Angle No. 3 at D's right hip.

2. With his left forearm, D carries out a block downwards and outwards to the right, while at the same time delivering a punch with the ball of the hand (disrupting action) at A's genitalia.

3. D brings his left arm clockwise round A's right arm, grabbing hold of A's neck with the right hand...

4. ...and pulling A's head towards the wall.

5. D turns A round further...

6. ...and brings A down to the ground with a twisting throw.

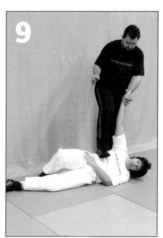

7. D disarms A with the left hand...

8. ...and brings the own right leg, bending it sharply, upwards.

9. D ends the combination with a downward kick at A's ribs.

22.2.2 D stands sideways to the wall (90°)

1. D stands sideways to the wall (with his left side nearer to the wall). A stands in front of D and strikes using Angle No. 1 (knife strike downwards from the outside at the neck).

2. With the right hand, D sweeps/brings the weapon-bearing arm diagonally downwards and outwards...

3. ...bringing it upwards further in a counter-clockwise direction (quasi in a circle)...

4. ...and smashes the weapon-bearing hand against the wall.

5. A delivers a left-handed punch at A's head. D loosens his hold on the right arm and brings the fingers of the right hand over A's eyes (clockwise)...

6. ...sweeps the left arm downwards and inwards with his left hand ...

7. ...and also then smashes the left hand against the wall. As he does this the left arm is lying over A's right arm so that A cannot make easy use of the knife. If A tries to cut, D presses the left arm upwards so that A cuts himself.

8. With the right hand, D brings the right weapon-bearing arm clockwise upwards and outwards and in the same movement grabs hold of the ball of A's thumb...

9. ...pulls the arm clockwise further downwards and again past his own body...

10. ...stretches out the left arm, places the blunt edge of the knife on his left forearm/upper arm...

11. ...pulls the weapon-bearing hand over the arm and disarms A. With the right hand, D is holding A's outstretched right arm. A delivers another left-handed punch at D's head.

12. D slides his left arm through under his right arm and sweeps/blocks the punch with the left hand counter-clockwise upwards in the direction of the wall, sweeping A's left arm with his right hand outwards again so that it is "opened"...

13. ...he then brings his right hand towards A's head...

14. ...grabs hold of A's neck with both hands...

15. ...and carries out a head butt at A's head.

22.3 Groundwork Techniques

22.3.1 A is in the mounted position on top of D

Angle No. 1 (Knife stab downwards and inwards from the outside at the neck)

1. A stabs using Angle No. 1 at the left side of D's neck.
2. With the left forearm, D carries out a block with the edge of the hand (Palm down block) upwards and outwards, while at the same time delivering a right-handed punch at A's genitalia...

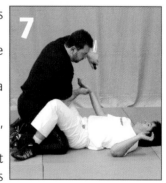

3. ...and grabs hold of the right wrist with his left hand, turns it round counter-clockwise so that the flat, blunt side of the knife is lying on his left forearm and the knife is pointing upwards. D pulls both of his feet up near to his bottom...
4. ...places the right hand on A's left hip, lifts up his hips...
5. ...and, over the left shoulder, turns A onto his back.

6. With the right hand, D grabs hold of the ball of A's right thumb, places the little finger of his left hand on A's little finger...

7. ...and disarms A with the left hand.

Angle No. 2 (Knife strike downwards and outwards from the inside at the neck)

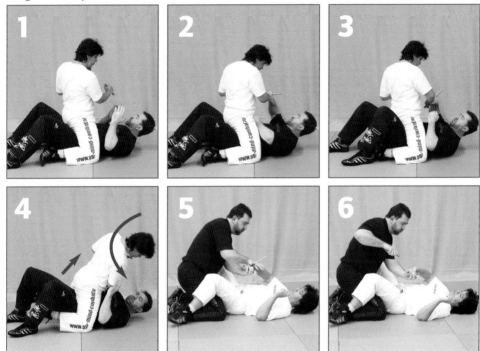

1. A is in the mounted position and strikes using Angle No. 2 (from the inside at the neck).

2. With a block using the edge of the right hand, D stops the attack, while at the same time delivering a left-handed punch at A's genitalia.

3. With the right hand, D grabs hold of A's wrist and turns it further clockwise. As he does this the flat, blunt side of the knife is lying on A's forearm. D pulls both of his feet up near to his bottom...

4. ... lifts up his hips...

5. ...turns A onto his back, grabs hold of the ball of A's right thumb with his left hand...

6. ...and disarms A with the right hand.

Angle No. 5 (Knife threat direct at the chest)

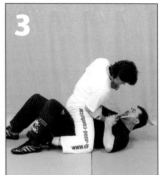

1. A is in the mounted position and places the knife on D's chest. Because the risk of a cut would be too high, D cannot strike/sweep the knife away.

2. With the left hand, D grabs hold of the ball of the right thumb of the weapon-bearing hand, presses the weapon-bearing arm close to his upper body so that A is not able to strike out, while at the same time delivering a punch at A's genitalia.

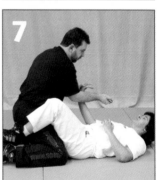

3. After that, D places his right hand on A's forearm (in order to prevent A pulling out the weapon-bearing arm), and pulls both of his feet up near to his bottom...

4. ...lifts up his hips...

5. ...and, over the left shoulder, turns A onto his back.

6. D turns A's weapon-bearing wrist counter-clockwise outwards to the left, places his thumb on the knife handle...

7. ...and disarms A with the hand.

Angle No. 5 (Knife stab downwards at the head)

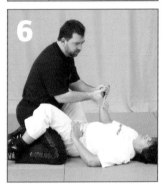

1. A is in the mounted position and stabs using Angle No. 5 (downwards at the head).
2. With the left hand, D sweeps the weapon-bearing arm clockwise outwards to the right...
3. ...and using A's weapon-bearing arm causes a self-inflicted wound on A's left thigh.
4. D pulls back the weapon-bearing arm counter-clockwise, places the right hand on the back of A's right hand...

5. ...carries out a bent hand lock...
6. ...and turns A onto his back. D places the right hand just above A's right hand...
7. ...and disarms A with the right hand.

22.3.2 A is kneeling between D's legs (Guard position)

Angle No. 1 (Knife stab downwards and inwards from the outside at the neck)

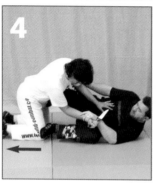

1. A is kneeling between D's legs (Guard position) and stabs using Angle No. 1 (from the outside at the neck).

2. With the left forearm, D carries out a block with the edge of the hand (Palm down block) upwards and outwards, while at the same time delivering a right-handed finger jab at A's eyes, grabbing hold of the right wrist with his left hand...

3. ...twists it round counter-clockwise so that the flat, blunt side of the knife is lying on his own left forearm and the knife is pointing upwards.
4. D rolls onto his left side, lifts up his hips to the right, places his left foot at A's right knee...
5. ...and kicks A's right leg backwards so that A falls down...
6. ...and turns A to the left onto his back.
7. With the right hand, D grabs hold of the ball of A's right thumb, places the little finger of the left hand on A's little finger...
8. ...and disarms A with the hand.

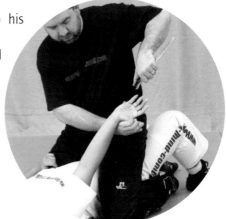

1. A is kneeling between D's legs (Guard position) and strikes using Angle No. 1 (from the outside at the neck).
2. With the left forearm, D carries out a block upwards and outwards, while at the same time delivering a right-handed finger jab at A's eyes.
3. With the right hand, D grabs hold of A's weapon-bearing arm...

4. ...and brings the weapon-bearing arm clockwise outwards to the right with his right hand,
also grabbing hold of A's right wrist with his left hand, rolling on to his right side...

5. ...sliding his left leg underneath A's head...

6. ...and immobilizes A using a twisting lever (stretched arm lock).

7. D places the little finger of the left hand on A's right hand.

8. In this position, D takes the knife off A with the right hand.

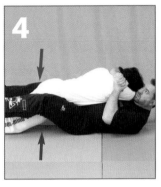

1. A is kneeling between D's legs and strikes using Angle No. 1 (from the outside at the neck).

2. With the left hand, D sweeps the attacking weapon-bearing arm from the outside to the inside...

3. ...and in the same movement brings his right arm over the left side of A's neck and grabs hold of his own right hand with his left hand.

4. D stretches out his legs and pins A's legs together with his thighs...

5. ...turning counter-clockwise to the left...

6. ...so that A is rolled over onto his back. D gets into the mounted position...

7. ...takes hold of A's right wrist with the left hand and carries out a stranglehold technique with his forearms.

187

Angle No. 2 (Knife strike downwards and outwards from the inside at the neck)

1. A is kneeling between D's legs and strikes using Angle No. 2 (inwards at the neck).
2. With the right hand, D carries out a block with the edge of the hand (Palm down block), while at the same time delivering a left-handed finger jab at A's eyes.
3. With the right hand, D grabs hold of A's wrist and turns it further round counter-clockwise. As he does this, the flat, blunt side of the knife is lying on D's forearm. D rolls onto his right side...
4. ...lifts up his own hips to the left, places his left shinbone in front of A's stomach and the right leg directly next to A's left leg.
5. D now carries out a scissors movement and turns A over to the right onto his back.
6. With the left hand, D grabs hold of the ball of A's right thumb, places the little finger on A's right hand...
7. ...and takes the knife off A with the right hand.

Angle No. 3 (Knife stab from the outside at waist level)

1. A is kneeling between D's legs and stabs using Angle No. 3 (from the outside at waist level).
2. With the left hand, D grabs hold of A's weapon-bearing wrist, while at the same time delivering a right-handed finger jab at A's eyes.
3. D lifts up his upper body, grasping over A's right arm with his right arm...
4. ...and grabbing hold of his own left wrist. D pushes his hips outwards to the left and presses A's bent arm in the direction of A's left shoulder (bent arm lock).

5. In this position, D loosens the right-handed grip on his own left hand, places the little finger close to the knife handle and on A's right hand...
6. ...and disarms A with the right hand.

Angle No. 4 (Knife stab inwards at waist level)

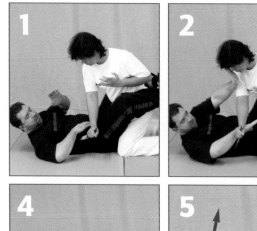
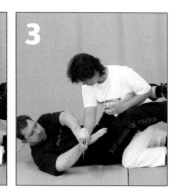

1. A is kneeling between D's legs (Guard position) and stabs using Angle No. 4 (inwards at waist level).

2. With the right forearm, D carries out a block upwards and outwards, while at the same time delivering a left-handed finger jab (disrupting action) at A's eyes.

3. With the left hand, D grabs hold of A's weapon-bearing wrist...

4. ...and twists the weapon-bearing arm round so that the little finger is facing upwards, then he rolls on to the right side of his body...

5. ...pushes the left leg in front of A's face and immobilizes him using a twisting lever (stretched arm lock).

6. In this position, D disarms A with the right hand.

Angle No. 5 (Knife threat - pointing at the middle of the upper body)

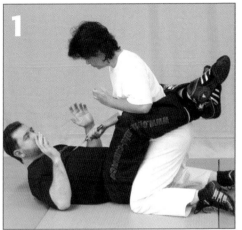
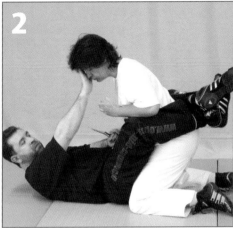

1. A is kneeling between D's legs (Guard position) and places the knife on D's chest. Because the risk of a cut would be too high, D cannot strike/sweep the knife away.
2. With the right hand, D grabs hold of A's weapon-bearing wrist, bends A's right hand so that the blade points towards A's upper body, while at the same time delivering a left-handed finger jab (disrupting action) at A's eyes.
3. D brings the knife over the right side of A's upper body (at liver height) on to A's back...
4. ...placing it in the region of the kidneys...
5. ...and pulls the hand forwards very close to A's upper body and disarms D over A's upper body.

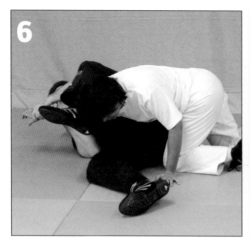

6. With the left hand, D grabs hold of A's weapon-bearing wrist, twists the weapon-bearing arm round
   so that the little finger is facing upwards, rolls onto the right side of his body...

7. ...pushes the left leg in front of A's face and immobilizes him using a twisting lever (stretched arm lock). In this position, D disarms A with the right hand.

Angle No. 5 (Knife stab downwards at the head)

1. A is kneeling between D's legs (Guard position) and stabs using Angle No. 5 (downwards at the head).

2. With the left hand, D carries out a block with the edge of the hand (Palm down block) upwards and outwards, while at the same time delivering a right-handed finger jab at A's eyes...

3. ...grabs hold of the right wrist with his left hand, twisting the wrist counter-clockwise so that the flat, blunt side of the knife is lying on his left forearm with the knife pointing upwards, while at the same time continuing to threaten A's right eye with a right-handed finger jab.

4. D rolls onto his left side lifts up his hips to the right, places the left foot on A's right knee...

5. ...kicks A's right leg backwards so that A falls down...

6. ...and turns A over to the left onto his back.

7. With the right hand, D grabs hold of the ball of A's right thumb, places the little finger of the left hand on A's little finger...

8. ...and takes the knife out of the hand.

23 Attack with the Knife in the Dagger Position

Angle No. 1 (Knife stab downwards and inwards from the outside at the neck)

1. A stabs using Angle No. 1 (inwards from the outside at the neck).

2. With the left hand, D carries out a block with the edge of the hand (Palm down block) upwards and outwards, while at the same time delivering a right-handed finger jab at A's eyes...

3. ...grabbing hold of the right wrist with his left hand...

4. ...and twists the wrist round counter-clockwise so that the flat, blunt side of the knife is lying on his left forearm with the knife pointing upwards.

Note: D could continue to sweep the weapon-bearing arm counter-clockwise outwards to the right. With this movement the disarming would be done automatically.

5. With the right hand, D grabs hold of A's right forearm...

6. ...and carries out a twisting motion with both hands in a counter direction (as if he is wringing out a towel). In this movement, the left forearm presses the flat, blunt side of the knife downwards. Thus, D disarms A with the forearm.

Note: Instead of disarming using the left forearm, D could act as follows:

- With the right hand, D grabs hold of the right thumb and places the edge of the left hand on the flat, blunt side of the knife.

- With the palm of the hand, D presses against the flat, blunt side of the knife (D places the edge of the hand close to A's hand and pressure is applied towards the ground).

- D places the left hand close to A's right hand so that the little fingers touch each other...

...thus executing the disarming action.

Unarmed Follow-on techniques:

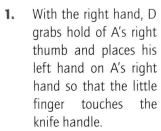

1. With the right hand, D grabs hold of A's right thumb and places his left hand on A's right hand so that the little finger touches the knife handle.
2. With the left hand, D presses against the knife handle...
3. ...and disarms A.
4. D pulls A's arm further forwards...
5. ...and gets behind A's back...

6. ...swinging the right arm round A's neck and placing his own right hand on his own left shoulder...

7. ...then slides the left hand behind A's head (with the back of the hand facing the back of A's head)...

8. ...and immobilizes A using a stranglehold technique (Mata Leao).

Follow-on technique using the weapon when D has disarmed A:

1. With the right hand, D grabs hold of the ball of A's right thumb and places the left hand on top of A's right hand...

2. ...and disarms A. After this, D holds the knife in a dagger position (ice pick position).

3. D pulls A's arm further forwards and gets round behind A's back...

4. ...placing the blade above A's left collarbone and holding A's right arm with his right hand...

5. ...and forces A down to the ground by pulling the knife backwards.

1. A stabs using Angle No. 1 (inwards from the outside at the neck).
2. With the left arm, D carries out a block outwards, while at the same time delivering a right-handed finger jab at A's eyes.
3. D swings his right arm through under the weapon-bearing arm (like a bent arm lock)...
4. ...and brings his arm upwards behind the weapon-bearing arm.
5. D places the left hand on the flat, blunt side of the knife and disarms A, turns him round further and can carry out either a stabbing technique, e.g. at the kidneys, or a control technique using the knife.

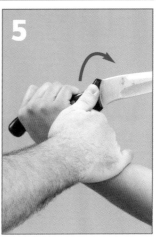

1. A stabs using Angle No. 1 (inwards from the outside at the neck).
2. With the right forearm, D takes up the weapon-bearing arm...
3. ...and at first sweeps it counter-clockwise downwards to the right...
4. ...and upwards to the right (making a circular motion of about 360°) and then places his own right thumb on the flat, blunt side of the knife (see detail)...
5. ...and disarms A using the circular motion mentioned above and applying pressure on the flat, blunt side of the knife with his thumb.

Angle No. 2 (Knife strike downwards and outwards from the inside at the neck)

1. A stabs using Angle No. 2 (from the inside at the neck).

2. With the left hand, D sweeps A's right weapon-bearing arm clockwise downwards, while at the same time delivering a right-handed finger jab (disrupting action) at A's eyes...

3. ...grabs hold of the ball of A's thumb with his right hand...

4. ...and grabs hold of A's forearm with his left arm). As he does this, the flat, blunt side of the knife is lying on D's left forearm.

5. With both hands, D carries out a twisting motion in a counter direction (as if he is wringing out a towel). In this movement, the left forearm presses the flat, blunt side of the knife downwards. Thus, D disarms A using the forearm.

Note: Instead of disarming using the left forearm, D could act as follows:

- D places the edge of the left hand on the flat, blunt side of the knife.
- With the palm of the hand, D presses against the flat, blunt side of the knife (D places the edge of the hand close to A's hand and pressure is applied towards the ground).
- D places the left hand close to A's right hand so that the little fingers touch each other.

...thus executing the disarming action.

Unarmed Follow-on techniques:

1. D pulls A's right arm further forwards...
2. ...gets round behind A's back...
3. ...and swings the right arm round A's neck placing his own right hand on his own left shoulder...
4. ...and slides the left hand behind A's head (with the back of the hand facing the back of A's head)...
5. ...and immobilizes A using a stranglehold technique (Mata Leao).

Follow-on technique using the weapon when D has disarmed A:

1. With the right hand, D is holding onto A's right thumb and places the left hand on top of A's right hand...
2. D disarms A with the left hand...
3. ...pulls A's arm further forwards and gets round behind A's back...
4. ...placing the blade above A's left collarbone and holding A's right arm with his right hand...
5. ...and forcing A down to the ground by pulling the knife backwards.

1. A stabs using Angle No. 2 (from the inside at the neck).
2. With the right hand, D sweeps the weapon-bearing arm further counter-clockwise upwards and inwards...
3. ...and immediately diagonally back again...
4. ...downwards and outwards to the right.
5. With the left hand, D grabs hold of A's right thumb and twists the hand round counter-clockwise back onto the left side.
6. D places the right hand on top of A's right hand so that D's and A's little fingers touch each other.
7. D disarms A with the right hand. After this, D has the knife in the dagger position.

8. D places the blade just above A's elbow, twists the right arm round clockwise inwards...

9. ...and carries out a twisting arm lock. As he does this, the knife is placed on the left side of A's neck.

10. D pulls at A's outstretched right arm and presses A's head clockwise downwards and inwards...

11. ...and brings A down to the ground with a twisting throw.

12. D carries out a right-footed kick at the right side of A's upper body...

13. ...places the leg over A and turns A over onto his stomach.

14. D immobilizes A on the ground with a stretched arm lock over the left thigh.

1. A stabs using Angle No. 2 (from the inside at the neck).
2. D stops the attack with a chop on A's weapon-bearing arm using both arms.
3. With the right hand, D grabs hold of A's wrist and twists it further round clockwise. As he does this, the flat, blunt side of the knife is lying on D's forearm.
4. D places the left hand from the outside on the little finger of A's right hand...
5. ...and disarms A with the left hand. After this, D holds the knife in the dagger position.

Angle No. 3 (Knife stab from the outside at waist level)

1. A stabs using Angle No. 3 (from the outside at waist level).
2. With the right forearm, D takes up the weapon-bearing arm...
3. ...sweeps it counter-clockwise upwards to the right (making a circular motion of about 270°) and then places his right thumb on the flat, blunt side of the knife...
4. ...and disarms A using the circular motion mentioned above and applying pressure on the flat, blunt side of the knife with his thumb.

1. A stabs using Angle No. 3 (from the outside at waist level).
2. With the right forearm, D takes up the weapon-bearing arm, while at the same time delivering a left-handed finger jab at A's eyes.
3. D sweeps the weapon-bearing arm counter-clockwise upwards to the right (making a circular motion of about 270°)...
4. ...and then takes the knife out of A's hand...
5. ...carries out another little circular motion counter-clockwise round A's right wrist...
6. ...places the blade on the wrist joint and the left hand on the top of the back of A's right hand and carries out a bent hand lock this way.

1. A stabs using Angle No. 3 (from the outside at waist level).
2. With his left forearm, D carries out a block downwards and outwards, while at the same time delivering a blow with his right elbow (disrupting action) forwards at A's right biceps.
3. D bends the right arm downwards...
4. ...and places the right hand on top of A's right hand...
5. ...twists A's outstretched arm clockwise outwards to the right, placing the left thumb on the knife handle...
6. ...and disarms A with the left hand.
7. D places the blade on A's elbow joint and pulls the elbow outwards to the left, bending A's arm and wrist so that the shape of a "Z" is formed and immobilzes A using a twisting hand lock.

Angle No. 4 (Knife stab from the inside at waist level)

1. A stabs using Angle No. 4 (from the inside at waist level).
2. With his right forearm, D carries out a block downwards and outwards to the right, while at the same time delivering a left-handed finger jab (disrupting action) at A's eyes.
3. With the left hand, D grabs hold of the ball of A's right thumb...
4. ...brings A's right hand counter-clockwise outwards to the left, places the little finger of the right hand on the little finger of A's right hand...
5. ...and disarms A with the right hand.
6. D bends A's right arm, places the blade on the outside of the elbow joint, and pulls A's right elbow counter-clockwise upwards...

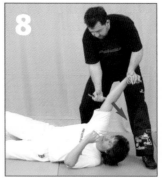

7.   ...and forces A using a bent arm lock down to the ground.

8.   D places the blade on top of A's right elbow...

9.   ...turns A over onto his stomach (by pulling the hand and pressing the blade against the elbow) and kneels down with the right leg on A's back, ending the combination with a stretched arm lock on the ground.

1.   A stabs using Angle No. 4 (from the inside at waist level).

2.   With his right forearm, D carries out a block downwards and outwards to the right, while at the same time delivering a left-handed finger jab (disrupting action) at A's eyes.

3.   With the left forearm, D presses against A's right upper arm so that A is not able to cut in his direction, and quickly grabs hold of the ball of A's right thumb with the hand...

4. ...brings the weapon-bearing arm clockwise outwards to the left...

5. ...places the left forearm on the flat, blunt side of the knife and grabs hold of A's right forearm with the left hand from below.

6. Now with both hands, D carries out a twisting motion in a counter direction as if he is wringing out a towel. By applying pressure with the left forearm against the blade the disarming action is carried out.

7. With his left arm, D brings the right arm counter-clockwise upwards and outwards...

8. ...and then he grabs hold of A's larynx with the right hand, placing the left hand in the area of A's loin...

9. ...and forces A down to the ground...

10. ...and immobilizes him with a stranglehold on the larynx.

1. A stabs Angle No. 4 (from the inside at waist level).

2. With the left hand, D carries out a sweeping action clockwise outwards to the left, while at the same time delivering a right-handed finger jab (disrupting action) at A's eyes...

3. ...then grabs hold of A's wrist (the ball of the right thumb) with the right hand...

4. ...bends it and places the little finger on A's little finger...

5. ...and disarms A with the left hand.

6. D gets round behind A but continues to hold A's right hand firmly with his right hand, places the knife point just above A's left collarbone...

7. ...and forces A down to the ground by pulling the knife backwards.

Angle No. 5 (Knife stab downwards at the head/upper body)

1. A stabs Angle No. 5 (downwards at the head).

2. With the left hand, D takes up the weapon-bearing arm...

3. ...brings it further downwards at A's thigh to cause a self-inflicted wound

4. ...pulls the arm upwards again (nearly to face level) so that the knife is pointing horizontally to the right (seen from A).

5. Now, D has the following alternatives to carry out the disarming:
He could apply pressure with the edge of the right hand against the flat, blunt side of the knife...

6. He could apply pressure with the ball of the right thumb against the flat, blunt side of the knife...

7. He could bring his right arm clockwise around A's right arm, stretch out the right hand upwards in order to pull A's bent right arm further upwards and place the ball of the thumb on the flat, blunt side of the knife.

8. With one of these techniques, D disarms A.

9. With the left hand, D brings A's right arm clockwise outwards...

10. ...carries out a right-fisted punch at A's head...

11. ...and a left-handed uppercut at A's head...

12. ...D takes a step backwards with the left leg at an angle of at least 90° to A...

13. ...and ends the combination with a low kick at the inside of A's right thigh.

1.   A stabs Angle No. 5 (downwards at the head).
2.   With the left hand, D takes up the weapon-bearing arm...
3.   ...brings it further downwards at A's right thigh to cause a self-inflicted wound...

4.   ...pulls the arm a little upwards again, places the right hand on top of A's right hand so that the little finger touches the knife handle...
5.   ...and disarms A with the right hand...
6.   ...places the knife on the elbow joint...
7.   ...in order to start a crossover grip (bent arm lock)...
8.   ...gets round behind A and places the knife on the left side of A's neck to keep him under control. With a crossover grip (bent arm lock as a "transporting lever") he moves A along.

1. A stabs Angle No. 5 (downwards at the head).
2. With the left hand, D takes up the weapon-bearing arm, while at the same time delivering a right-handed finger jab at A's eyes...
3. ...and brings A's right arm downwards at A's thigh to cause a self-inflicted wound.
4. D places the blade on the inside of A's thigh...
5. ...pulls the hand outwards to the left and thus disarms A over his thigh.
6. D brings the outstretched arm further to the left...
7. ...and ends the combination with a reverse body lock (stretched arm lock).

216

24 More Angles

In many self-defense systems Angles 1-5 are identical, but others are different or are partially non-existent. For this reason we have numbered the other attack angles and have described their execution.

Angle No. 6 (Knife stab from the outside at the left side of the chest)

1. At chest height, A delivers a stab from the right straight at the left side of D's chest.

2. D carries out a block with the edge of the hand upwards and outwards to the left, while at the same time delivering a right-handed finger jab (disrupting action) at the head and taking a lunging step 45° forwards to the right.

3. D places the right forearm underneath A's right upper arm...

4. ...and with the right hand, brings the weapon-bearing arm clockwise upwards...

5. ...and further downwards to the right until the knife points at the ground. As he does this, D takes a step backwards with the right leg, grabs hold of the ball of the thumb with the right hand, places the edge of the left hand on the flat, blunt side of the knife...

6. ...and disarms A with the edge of the hand.

7. D places his left forearm on top of A's right forearm...

8. ...presses his forearm at an angle of about 45° downwards (towards himself), while at the same time delivering a head butt at A's head.

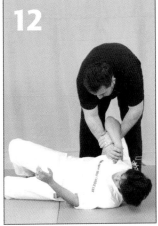

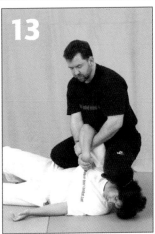

9. D brings his left arm clockwise round A's right arm...

10. ...grabs hold of his own right wrist...

11. ...and in the same movement, carries out a blow with the elbow forwards at A's head...

12. ...and forces A down to the ground using a bent arm lock.

13. D immobilizes A on the ground using a bent hand lock. To do this, D kneels down at the right side of A's upper body.

1. A delivers a stab at chest height from the right straight at the left side of D's chest.

2. D places the right forearm on A's right forearm...

3. ...and brings the weapon-bearing arm diagonally counter-clockwise inwards with the right hand, while at the same time delivering a left-handed finger jab (disrupting action) at A's eyes...

4. ...then grabs hold of the ball of A's right thumb with the left hand...

5. ...places the right forearm on the flat, blunt side of the knife...

6. ...and disarms A with the right forearm.

7. With the right arm, D carries out a bent arm lock...

8. ...and places the left hand on the right side of A's head.

Angle No. 7 (Knife stab from the inside at the right side of the chest)

1. At chest height, A delivers a knife stab from the left at the right side of D's chest.
2. D counters with a block using the edge of the hand upwards and outwards to the right, while at the same time delivering a left-handed finger jab (disrupting action) at the head and taking a lunging step 45° forwards to the left.
3. D places the left forearm on top of A's right forearm...
4. ...sweeps the weapon-bearing arm clockwise downwards and outwards to the left with his left hand...
5. ...grabs hold of the weapon-bearing hand with the right hand...
6. ...and twists it clockwise further to the right, applying a twisting hand lock...

7. ...places the left hand above A's right hand so that D's hand touches the knife handle...
8. ...and disarms A with the left hand.

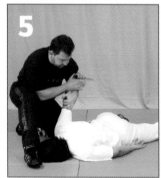

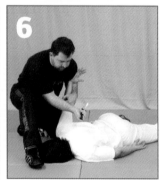

1. At chest height, A delivers a knife stab from the left at the right side of D's chest.
2. D counters with a left-handed sweeping action clockwise downwards and outwards to the left, while at the same time delivering a finger jab at A's eyes...
3. ...brings his left arm clockwise around A's right arm...
4. ...applies a twisting arm lock (stretched arm lock) and presses A's head at an angle of about 45° forwards to the ground with his right hand.
5. D immobilizes A with a twisting arm lock.
6. D disarms A with the right hand.

Angle No. 8 (Knife strike horizontally across the chest/neck)

The strike is delivered horizontally from the left to the right across the chest or neck.

1. A delivers a strike horizontally from the left to the right across D's chest.
2. D counters with a block using the edge of the hand upwards and outwards to the right, while at the same time delivering a left-handed finger jab (disrupting action) at A's eyes and taking a lunging step 45° forwards to the left.
3. With the right hand, D grabs hold of A's right wrist, brings his own left arm clockwise round A's weapon-bearing arm...
4. ...grabs hold of his own right wrist...
5. ...turns in A's direction, and carries out in the same movement a blow with the elbow upwards at A's head...

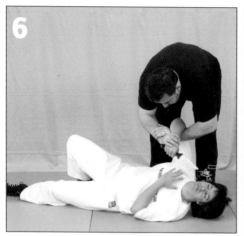

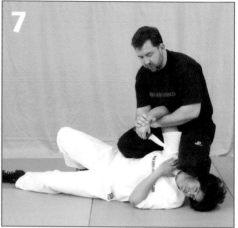

6. ...and forces A down to the ground using a bent arm lock.

7. With both knees, D kneels down at the right side of A's upper body, applies a bent hand lock...

8. ...places the left hand above A's right hand...

9. ...and disarms A.

1.   A delivers a strike horizontally from the left to the right across D's chest.

2.   D counters with a left-handed sweeping action clockwise downwards and outwards to the left, while at the same time delivering a finger jab at A's eyes...

3.   ...brings the weapon-bearing arm further outwards to the left...

4.   ...takes a step forwards with the right leg, grabs hold of the wrist (of the weapon-bearing hand) with the right hand...

5.   ...and immobilizes A using a reverse body lock.

6.   D disarms A with the right hand.

Angle No. 9 (Knife strike/stab diagonally upwards and inwards from the right)

The strike/stab is delivered at hip height diagonally from the right (seen from D) at A's right shoulder.

1. At hip height, A delivers a strike from the right diagonally upwards and inwards to the left.
2. D counters with a right-handed sweeping action counter-clockwise outwards to the right, while at the same time delivering a left-handed finger jab at A's eyes.
3. D places his left hand underneath A's right elbow...
4. ...and delivers a right-handed finger jab at A's eyes.

5. With the right hand, D grabs hold of the ball of A's right thumb...

6. ...brings the weapon-bearing hand clockwise towards A's liver...

7. ...brings the weapon-bearing hand over the right side of A's upper body, places the flat, blunt side of the knife on A's back in the region of the kidneys...

8. ...pulls the weapon-bearing arm along forwards close to A's body and disarms A over the body.

Angle No. 10 (Knife strike/stab diagonally upwards and outwards from the left)

The strike/stab is delivered at hip height diagonally from the left (seen from D) at A's left shoulder.

1. At hip height, A delivers a strike from the left diagonally upwards and outwards to the right.
2. With the left hand, D sweeps the weapon-bearing arm counter-clockwise upwards...
3. ...and further outwards to the left...
4. ...then again inwards (nearly 360°)...
5. ...and grabs hold of the ball of A's right thumb with the right hand...

6. ...and A's right forearm with the left hand.

7. D forces a knife stab at the right side of A's upper body...

8. ...pulls the knife back again...

9. ...places the right hand underneath A's right hand and on the flat, blunt side of the knife...

10. ...and disarms A with the hand.

25 Self-defense with the Knife against Contact Attacks

This section deals with the situation where the defender has disarmed the attacker in an armed conflict. The attacker then tries to bar the defender from using the knife for defense and grabs hold of the weapon-bearing arm or clinches the defender's arms. In these examples, the defender only uses the knife to control the attacker. Only in exceptional cases, should the knife be used for striking or stabbing.

25.1 Bear hug from the Side Trapping the Arms

1. D holds the knife in the normal position. With both arms, A hugs round D over his arms from the side so that D cannot use the knife for defense.
2. D brings the knife round A's back...
3. ...and also grabs hold of the knife handle with the left hand...
4. ...tightens the grip and pulls it upwards so that A comes forwards...

5. ...pulls A's body onto his hip...
6. ...and executes a hip throw.

25.2 Grabbing Hold of the Diagonally Opposite Wrist

1. D holds the knife in the dagger position. With the right hand, A grabs hold of D's right weapon-bearing wrist.
2. With the left hand, D holds A's fingers against his wrist...
3. ...brings the blade over A's wrist from the outside...
4. ...and applies a twisting hand lock (Z-Lock).

1. D holds the knife in the normal position. With the right hand, A grabs hold of D's right wrist (weapon-bearing hand).

2. With the right diagonal hand, D grabs hold of A's right wrist (weapon-bearing wrist), while at the same time delivering a foot kick (disrupting technique) at A's right shinbone.

3. D turns further round clockwise. With the left hand, D grabs hold of A's right wrist.

4. D levers A's outstretched arm over the left side of his upper body so that A is forced to move forward. As he does this, D carries out a grip release technique with the right hand...

5. ...takes a step turn 180° and places the knife handle on top of the back of A's right hand.

6. D executes a twisting hand lock in connection with a step turn...

7. ...and forces A down to the ground with it.

25.3 Grabbing the Opposite Wrist

1. D holds the knife in the dagger position. With the left hand, A grabs hold of D's opposite right wrist.
2. With the left hand, D grabs hold of A's left wrist and holds it against his own wrist.
3. D twists his forearm so that the knife is pointing at A. D presses his right forearm against A's hand and controls him with a twisting hand lock.

1. D holds the knife in the dagger position. With the left hand, A grabs hold of D's opposite right wrist.
2. With the left hand, D grabs hold of A's left wrist, delivers a foot kick at A's shinbone...
3. ...turns A's left hand counter-clockwise inwards...
4. ...and brings the knife from the outside round A's arm. In this position, D immobilizes A using a left-handed twisting hand lock.

25.4   Grabbing Hold of Both Wrists from Behind

1. D holds the knife in the dagger position. With both hands, A grabs hold of D's wrists from behind.
2. D pulls his right leg upwards...
3. ...and kicks at A's right knee with full power...
4. ...bringing his right elbow downwards...
5. ...pushes the right arm hard forwards and carries out a grip release technique.
6. D turns to the left, carries out a Tan-Sao with the left arm...
7. ...grabs hold of A's left wrist with the left hand employing a form of grip release technique...

8. ...brings the left arm behind A's back (bent arm lock)...

9. ...and, from behind, places the point of the knife point just to the rear of A's right collarbone.

1. D holds the knife in the dagger position. With both hands, A grabs hold of D's wrists from behind.

2. D brings his left elbow downwards...

3. ...carries out a grip release technique with the left hand...

4. ...takes a step turn 180°...

5. ...holds the fingers of A's right hand against his own right wrist, brings the blade over A's right wrist...

6. ...and controls A using a twisting hand lock (Z-Lock).

25.5 Grabbing Hold of Both Wrists from the Front

1. With the right hand, D holds the knife in the dagger position. A stands in front of D and grabs hold of both wrists.
2. D presses the wrists together.
3. A reacts against it and presses the wrists outwards.
4. D takes advantage of this reaction and dives through under A's left arm. Thus, D breaks the grip on the weapon-bearing hand. D presses against A's left upper arm with the neck so that A is not able to carry out a stranglehold technique.
5. Now, in an emergency situation, D can stab at A's back or can control A with the knife in the region of the kidneys.

1. With the right hand, D holds the knife in the dagger position. A stands in front of D and grabs hold of both wrists.
2. D lifts up the left leg...
3. ...and executes a knee kick just underneath A's left wrist (grip release technique).
4. D brings the blade behind A's right upper arm...
5. ...pulls A's right arm inwards...
6. ...and ends the combination using a left-fisted punch at A's head.

25.6 Grabbing Hold of the Weapon-bearing Wrist with Both Hands

1. With the right hand, D holds the knife in the dagger position. With both hands, A grabs hold of D's weapon-bearing wrist.
2. D carries out a right-footed kick at A's right shinbone...
3. ...pulls the right arm against A's thumbs...
4. ...carries out a grip release technique (in the direction of the thumbs) upwards towards his left shoulder...
5. ...places the blade from the outside just above A's right arm, brings the right arm inwards...
6. ...places the blade on the left side of A's neck from behind and presses the right arm against the right side of A's neck. D holds onto A's right arm with the left hand.

26 Counter Measures and Follow-on Techniques after Knife Attacks

Starting position: A holds the knife in the dagger position (ice pick position - blade on the side of the little finger).

1. A stabs using Angle No. 1 (at the right side of D's neck).
2. With the left hand, D takes up the attack, while at the same time delivering a right-handed finger jab at A's eyes...
3. ...places the right forearm on top of A's right forearm...
4. ...brings the knife hand further immediately clockwise downwards and outwards with the right hand...
5. ...rolls his own right hand round the wrist holding the knife...
6. ...so that he can disarm A using the hand by applying pressure with the right thumb on the flat, blunt side of the knife.

Counter Measure Technique

1. As soon as D carries out the block with his left forearm, A bends the knife round D's left arm...
2. ...pulls D's arm outwards and delivers a horizontal cut across D's chest.
3. A pulls his weapon-bearing arm further to the left.

Follow-on Technique

1. With the free right hand, D wards off the strike at the neck...

2. ...and with the right hand immediately brings the knife hand further clockwise downwards and outwards...
3. ...rolls his own right hand round the wrist holding the knife...
4. ...so that he can disarm A using the hand by applying pressure with the right thumb on the flat, blunt side of the knife.

Counter Measure Technique

1. Before D is able to carry out the disarming action...
2. ...A presses D's right arm further upwards and outwards to the left.
3. A knife stab at the spleen is applied as a closing technique.

Follow-on Technique

1. When A presses D's right arm upwards with his left forearm...

2. ...and tries to carry out a right-handed stab...
3. ...D forestalls with the left hand (before the sweeping action is carried out) and immobilizes A's left arm with the forearm by applying pressure upwards...
4. ...and, with his right hand sweeps the right knife hand downwards and outwards to the right, and with his left hand A's left hand outwards to the left.

5. D carries out a stretched arm lock with A's left arm and presses A's bent right arm over A's left elbow.

Counter Measure Technique

1. A counters D's right-handed sweeping action...
2. ...by circling with the knife (before the sweeping action is carried out) counter-clockwise round the arm...
3. ...and pulling the arm upwards...
4. ...bringing the left arm crosswise downwards to the right arm...
5. ...and, again, circling the knife over the arm so that he can control both arms with the knife.
6. A pulls D's left hand so that a stretched arm lock is carried out. This can also be done without holding the arms beforehand.

27 Training Methods and Exercises (Drills) Exercises (Drills): Unarmed Against a Knife

27.1 Disarming drills

1. A holds the knife in the right hand (dagger position) and carries out Angle No. 1 (from the outside at the neck).
2. With the left hand, D takes up the weapon-bearing arm (blocking with the forearm upwards and outwards to the left), while at the same time delivering a right-handed finger jab (disrupting technique) at A's eyes...
3. ...places the right forearm underneath A's right forearm...
4. ...and brings it clockwise outwards to the right with the right hand...
5. ...grabs hold of the ball of A's right thumb with the right hand...
6. ...places the left hand on the flat, blunt side of the knife...

7. ...and executes a disarming action using the left hand.

8. With the left hand, D stabs (in the dagger position) Angle No. 1 (from the outside at the neck).

9. A carries out a left-handed jab at the neck

and simultaneously, with the right hand, a passive block outwards to the right.

10. ...and grabs hold of the left forearm (near D's wrist) with the right hand...

11. ...and twists the arm clockwise outwards so that the flat, blunt side of the knife is laying close on the forearm...

12. ...takes hold of the hand (ball of the thumb) with the left hand...

13. ...and places the right hand near to D's weapon-bearing hand...

14. ...and disarms D using the right hand so that the knife is again in the dagger position.

15. With the right hand, A stabs using Angle No. 3 (from the outside at waist level).

16. With the right hand, D carries out a sweeping action counter-clockwise, while at the same time delivering a left-handed jab at A's eyes...

17. ...brings the weapon-bearing arm further outwards to the right with the right hand...

18. ...and grabs hold of the ball of A's right thumb with the left hand...

19. ...places the right hand near to D's weapon-bearing hand so that the little finger is laying directly behind D's little finger...

20. ...and executes the disarming action using the right hand so that afterwards the knife is again in the dagger position.

21. With the right hand, A stabs using Angle No. 2 (from the inside at the neck).

22. With both forearms, D "blocks" the weapon-bearing arm...

23. ...grabbing hold of A's knife wrist with the right hand and twisting the arm into the form of a twisting hand lock (Z-Lock) so that the knife is laying again close to his own forearm.

24. The left hand takes on the weapon-bearing hand by pulling A's little finger outwards.

25. The right hand carries out the disarming by pulling the knife away from the attacker.

26. First of all, D brings the knife backwards to the right...

27. ...round his head (Rendondo)...

28. ...and, with the right hand, stabs Angle No. 4 (from the inside at waist level) at A's right hip.

29. D carries out a block downwards and outwards to the right, while at the same time delivering a left-handed finger jab at the eyes.

30. With the left hand, D grabs hold of the ball of A's right thumb...

31. ...places the little finger against A's little finger...

32. ...and disarms using the right hand.

33. D stabs using Angle No. 5 from above (downwards at the head).

34. A takes a step to the rear with the right leg...

35. ...and brings the weapon-bearing arm further downwards with the left hand in D's direction to cause a self-inflicted wound on D's right leg.

36. After this, he pulls the arm upwards again and twists it...

37. ...supporting the movement by taking a step turn outwards...

38. ...and disarms using the right hand.

39. A stabs using Angle No. 2 (from the inside at the neck).

40. D's right hand or right arm is still stretched out and brings the knife hand counter-clockwise upwards and inwards...

41. ...further downwards in a circle...

42. ...and again inwards.

43. The left hand takes on the knife hand...

44. ...and the right hand carries out the disarming, this time so that the knife is on the side of the thumb.

45. D strikes using Angle No. 2 (from the inside at the neck).

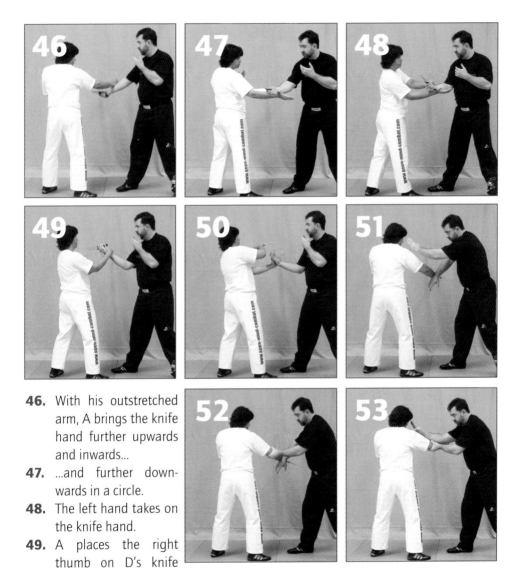

46. With his outstretched arm, A brings the knife hand further upwards and inwards...

47. ...and further downwards in a circle.

48. The left hand takes on the knife hand.

49. A places the right thumb on D's knife handle...

50. ...and the right hand carries out the disarming so that the knife is again in the dagger position.

51. A stabs using Angle No. 4 (from the outside at waist level). D carries out a right-handed block downwards and outwards, while at the same time delivering a left-handed finger jab at the eyes...

52. ...places the left hand underneath A's right elbow...

53. ...and delivers another finger jab at A's eyes with the right hand...

54. ...grabs hold of the ball of A's right thumb with the right hand...

55. ...and bringing the arm clockwise inwards...

56. ...and disarms A with the left hand so that D holds the knife in the normal position.

57. With the left hand, D strikes using Angle No. 3 (from the outside at waist level).

58. With the left hand, A sweeps the weapon-bearing arm clockwise inwards...

59. ...and further outwards to the left, while at the same time delivering a right-handed finger jab at the eyes.

60. With the right hand, A grabs hold of the ball of D's left thumb...

61. ...and brings the weapon-bearing hand clockwise outwards to the right...

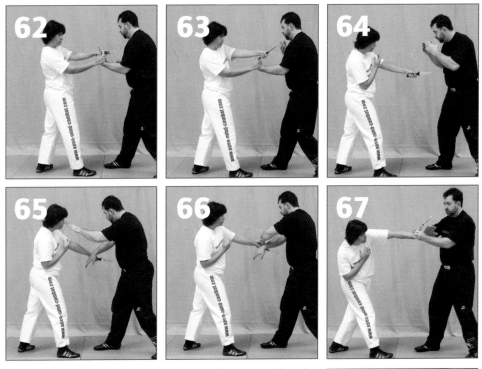

62. ...places the left hand above D's weapon-bearing hand...

63. ...and disarms D using the left hand so that A holds the knife in the normal position.

64. With the left hand, A stabs using Angle No. 5 at D's stomach.

65. With the right forearm, D carries out a block downwards and outwards to the right, while at the same time delivering a hand jab at A's eyes...

66. ...grabs hold of A's left hand with the left hand...

67. ...twists the wrist counter-clockwise upwards and inwards...

68. ...and carries out the disarming action using the right hand so that afterwards the knife is in dagger position (ice pick position).

Start all over again (with reversed roles)!

1. With the right hand, A stabs using Angle No. 2 in the dagger position (from the inside at the neck).

2. With the outstretched right hand, D brings the weapon-bearing hand counter-clockwise upwards and inwards...

3. ...further downwards...

4. ...and to the left downwards and outwards.

5. A pulls back the arm again...

6. ...and stabs using Angle No. 2 again (from the inside at the neck). D "blocks" with both forearms...

7. ...grabs hold of A's knife wrist with the right hand and twists the arm to form a twisting hand lock (Z-Lock). The knife lies close to his own forearm again...

8. The left hand takes on the weapon-bearing hand by controlling the ball of the thumb...

9. ...and the right hand carries out the disarming action by pulling the knife away from the attacker.

Start all over again (with reversed roles)!

1. With the right hand, A stabs using Angle No. 1 in the dagger position (from the outside at the neck).
2. D places the left hand underneath A's right arm...
3. ...and brings the knife hand inwards with the outstretched left arm.
4. A pulls back the right arm...
5. ...and stabs using Angle No. 2 in the dagger position (from the inside at the neck). D places the right hand underneath A's right arm...
6. ...bringing the knife hand inwards with the outstretched left arm...
7. ...and further counter-clockwise outwards to the right.

8. A pulls back the right arm...

9. ...and stabs using Angle No. 2 (from the inside at the neck).

10. D "blocks" with both forearms...

11. ...grabs hold of A's knife wrist with the right hand and twists the arm to form a twisting hand lock (Z-Lock). The knife lies close to his own forearm again...

12. The left hand takes on the weapon-bearing hand by controlling the ball of the thumb...

13. ...and the right hand carries out the disarming action by pulling the knife away from the attacker.

Start all over again (with reversed roles)!

27.2 Disrupting Techniques and Control of the Weapon-bearing Arm

1. A holds the knife in the normal position and strikes using Angle No. 1 (from the outside at the neck) at
the left side of D's neck.
2. With the left forearm, D carries out a block upwards and outwards to the left, while at the same time delivering a right-handed finger jab at A's eyes...
3. ...places the right forearm on top of A's right forearm...
4. ...sweeps A's weapon-bearing hand counter-clockwise downwards to the left with the right hand ...
5. ...and places the left arm underneath A's right elbow...
6. ...and delivers a finger jab at A's eyes.

7. A strikes using Angle No. 2 (from the inside at the neck).

8. D places the left hand underneath A's right elbow...

9. ...carries out a block upwards and outwards to the right with the right forearm...

10. ...and delivers another left-handed finger jab at A's eyes.

11. D places the left hand underneath A's right elbow, while at the same time delivering another right-handed finger jab at A's eyes.

12. With the right leg, A takes a step to the rear, and also pulls back the weapon-bearing hand...

13. ...and strikes using Angle No. 3 (from the outside at waist level).

14. D carries out a block downwards and outwards to the left, while at the same time delivering a right-handed finger jab at A's eyes...

15. ...places the right forearm on top of A's right forearm...

16. ...brings the weapon-bearing arm counter-clockwise downwards and outwards to the right with the right hand...

17. ...places the left hand underneath A's right elbow...

18. ...and delivers a right-handed finger jab at A's eyes.

19. A strikes using Angle No. 4 (from the inside at waist level).

20. D carries out a block downwards and outwards to the right and places the left hand underneath A's right elbow.

21. D delivers a right-handed finger jab at A's eyes...

22. ...A takes a step to the rear with the right leg, and also pulls back the weapon-bearing hand...

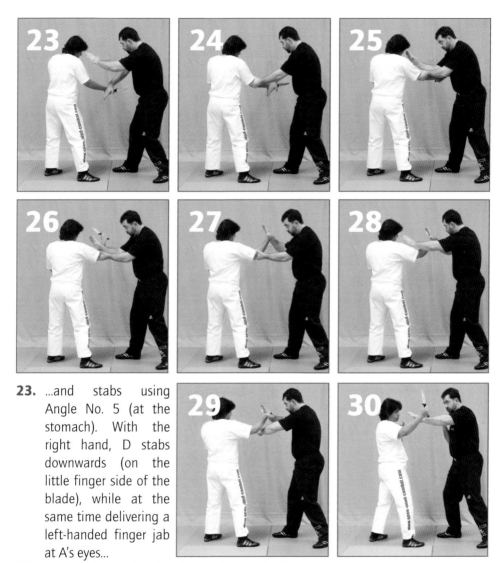

23. ...and stabs using Angle No. 5 (at the stomach). With the right hand, D stabs downwards (on the little finger side of the blade), while at the same time delivering a left-handed finger jab at A's eyes...

24. ...places the left hand underneath A's right elbow...

25. ...and delivers a right-handed finger jab at A's eyes.

26. A strikes using Angle No. 2 (from the inside at the neck).

27. D carries out a forearm block upwards and outwards to the right...

28. ...while at the same time delivering a left-handed finger jab at A's eyes.

29. D places the left hand underneath A's right arm...

30. ...and sweeps A's right arm counter-clockwise outwards to the left. This is expressly done this way so that A can begin once again with Angle No. 1.

Additional Disarming Action for the Previous Drill

After numbers 5, 11, 17, 20, and 24, the following disarming action can be incorporated for example:

1. With the right hand, D grabs hold of the ball of A's right thumb...
2. ...brings the weapon-bearing arm clockwise downwards to the left until the knife points at the ground, and then places the palm of the left hand facing upwards on the flat, blunt side of the knife (As he does this, D places his forefinger against A's forefinger)...
3. ...and carries out the disarming action with the left hand.

    Start all over again (with reversed roles)!

27.3 Loop Drills

In this exercise form, the function of the partner holding the knife can be compared to a ball machine at the tennis-court. A attacks again and again and tries to cut D. Thereby, D practices his sweeping, disrupting, and disarming techniques. After a defined number of repetitions a changeover of position should take place.

27.3.1 Basics

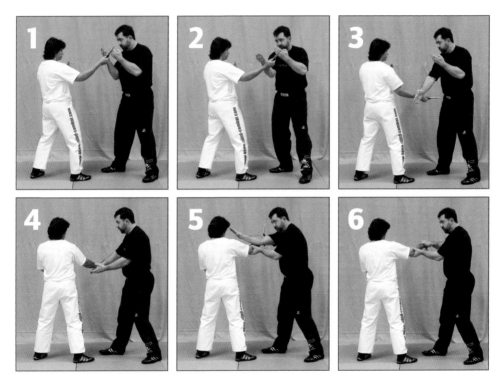

1. A holds the knife in the normal position and strikes using Angle No. 1 (from the outside at the neck).
2. With the right forearm, D takes on the knife and simultaneously in the same movement turns his body to the left and places his left leg rearwards (the right foot is forwards).
3. D brings the arm counter-clockwise outwards to the right, and places his left leg forwards and the right leg to the rear.
4. D places the left hand underneath A's right elbow...
5. ...slides the right hand over the right upper arm (at elbow level) and delivers a finger jab at A's eyes.
6. D places his right hand on top of A's right hand...

7. ...and brings the weapon-bearing arm clockwise outwards again to the left.
8. Finally, D takes hold of A's weapon-bearing arm with the left hand.

27.3.2 With an Additional Strike Using Angle No. 2

1. A holds the knife in the normal position and strikes using Angle No. 1 (from the outside at the neck).
2. With the right forearm, D takes on the knife and simultaneously in the same movement turns his body to the left and places his left leg rearwards (the right foot is forwards).
3. D brings the arm counter-clockwise outwards to the right...
4. ...places his left leg forwards and the right leg to the rear. A strikes using Angle No. 2 (from the inside at D's neck). With the left forearm, D takes on the knife...
5. ...brings the arm clockwise outwards to the left, and places his right leg forwards and the left leg to the rear.

27.3.3 Controlling the "Third Hand"

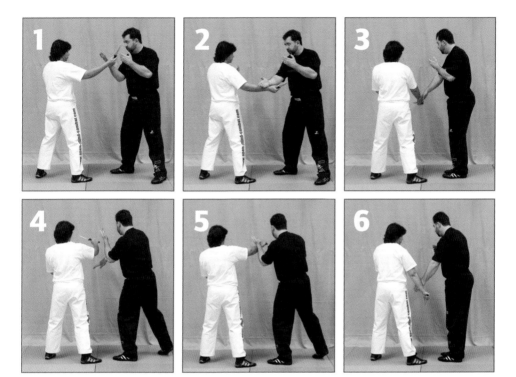

1. A holds the knife in the normal position and strikes using Angle No. 1 (from the outside at the neck).
2. With the right forearm, D takes on the knife and simultaneously in the same movement turns his body to the left and places his left leg rearwards (the right foot is forwards).
3. D brings the arm counter-clockwise outwards to the right, places his left leg forwards and the right leg to the rear.
4. A strikes using Angle No. 2 (from the inside at the neck).
5. D places the left hand on top of A's right forearm...
6. ...and brings the weapon-bearing arm clockwise outwards to the left. In doing so, D puts his right foot forwards.

7. D places his left leg to the rear and A delivers a left-fisted punch at D's head.

8. With the right hand, D sweeps A's left arm inwards.

27.3.4 Triple Tapping

Triple tapping is part of the follow-on techniques. The defender tries to carry out a sweeping action. The attacker prevents the use or rather sweeping action of the particular arm by striking it to the side for example. In this case, the defender follows up using the other arm and can still carry out the sweeping action. To develop this reaction, I have included an exercise form that builds up these abilities step by step.

Basic exercise

1. A holds the knife in the normal position and strikes using Angle No. 1 (from the outside at the neck).

2. With the right forearm, D takes on the knife and simultaneously in the same movement turns his body to the left and places his left leg rearwards (the right foot is forwards).

3. D brings the arm counter-clockwise outwards to the right...

4. ...places his left leg forwards and the right leg to the rear. A strikes using Angle No. 2 (from the inside at D's neck). With the left forearm, D takes on the knife...

5. ...brings the arm clockwise outwards to

the left and takes a step forwards with the right leg and a step to the rear with the left leg.

Phase 2

1. A holds the knife in the normal position and strikes using Angle No. 1.

2. With the right forearm, D takes on the knife and simultaneously in the same movement turns his body to the left and places his left leg rearwards (the right foot is forwards).

3. ...starts a sweeping action with his left forearm...

4. ...and then a sweeping action with his right hand...

5. D brings the arm counter-clockwise outwards to the right, places his left leg forwards...

6. ...and the right leg rearwards.

7. A strikes using Angle No. 2 (from the inside at D's neck). With the left forearm, D takes on the knife and simultaneously in the same movement turns his body to the right...

8. ...starts a sweeping action with his right forearm...

9. ...and then a sweeping action with his left hand.

10. D brings the arm clockwise outwards to the left, places his right leg forwards...

11. ...and the left leg to the rear.

Start over again...

266

Phase 3

1. A holds the knife in the normal position and strikes using Angle No. 1.
2. With the right forearm, D takes on the knife and simultaneously in the same movement turns his body to the left and places his left leg rearwards (the right foot is forwards).
3. A strikes D's right forearm away and prevents the sweeping action. D starts a left-handed sweeping action.
4. A strikes D's left forearm away and prevents the sweeping action. Then, D starts a right-handed sweeping action...
5. ...and brings the arm counter-clockwise outwards to the right.
6. A strikes using Angle No. 2 (from the inside at the neck). With the left forearm, D takes on the knife and simultaneously in the same movement turns his body to the right.
7. A strikes D's left forearm away and prevents the sweeping action.

8. D starts a right-handed sweep with the forearm.

9. A strikes D's right forearm away and prevents the sweeping action.

10. Then, D starts a left arm sweeping action...

11. ...bringing the arm clockwise outwards to the left.

When this sequence has been mastered, the footwork as described in Phase 2 can be incorporated.

Using Gunting Techniques

The term 'Gunting', translated means 'scissors'. Normally, a sweeping technique with one hand and a striking technique with the other hand is carried out at the same time.

1. A holds the knife in the normal position and strikes using Angle No. 1 with the right hand (from the outside at D's neck).
2. With the left hand, D brings the weapon-bearing hand clockwise inwards and carries out a right-fisted punch (Gunting) at the lower part of A's upper arm...
3. ...and, following on immediately, brings the knife back again clockwise...
4. ..and carries out a right-fisted punch at A's weapon-bearing hand.
5. With the left hand, D takes hold of A's weapon-bearing arm and the right hand is in a position to parry the next strike.

1. A holds the knife in the normal position and strikes using Angle No. 1 (from the outside at A's neck).

2. With the left hand D carries out a block with the edge of the hand (palm down block) upwards and outwards to the left, while at the same time delivering a hand jab at A's neck...

3. ...brings the weapon-bearing arm counter-clockwise downwards and inwards with the left hand...

4. ...and, in the same movement, carries out a right-fisted punch at A's biceps.

5. D brings the right arm further outwards to the left...

6. ...places the left forearm on top of A's right forearm...

7. ...and brings the weapon-bearing arm clockwise outwards to the left.

27.4 Exercises (Drills): Knife versus Knife

Drill 1

1. A holds the knife in the normal position and D holds his in the dagger position. A stabs using Angle No. 1 (from the outside at the neck).
2. D blocks the attack with the blade...
3. ...pulls the knife upwards...
4. ...and immediately hooks behind the weapon-bearing arm again...
5. ...and then brings the knife further downwards and inwards. As he does this, D puts his left leg forwards.
6. A strikes using Angle No. 2 (from the inside at the neck). D puts his right leg rearwards.
7. D stops the strike with the blade ...

8. ...brings the knife over A's weapon-bearing forearm...

9. ...and brings the weapon-bearing arm downwards and inwards to the left.

10. D places the left hand on A's right weapon-bearing arm.

11. Now, D stabs using Angle No. 5 (downwards at the head)...

12. With his own knife, A strikes D's right forearm and simultaneously sweeps the arm inwards to the right with the left hand...

13. ...and further clockwise downwards to the right.

14. With the left hand, D sweeps away A's left hand outwards.

Drill 2: Fivecount Sumbrada

1. A and D both hold the knife in the normal position.
2. A strikes using Angle No. 1 (inwards from the outside at D's neck) and takes a step forwards with the right leg. D strikes the weapon-bearing hand with the knife ...
3. ...and then controls the weapon-bearing hand with his left hand.
4. D strikes using Angle No. 4 (from the inside at A's stomach). A strikes the weapon-bearing hand downwards, while at the same time taking a step to the rear with the right leg.
5. A now controls the weapon-bearing hand with his left hand so that the palm of his hand is facing upwards.
6. A stabs using Angle No. 5 (at D's stomach). D strikes the weapon-bearing arm upwards...
7. ...controls the weapon-bearing arm with his left hand...

8.   ...and strikes using Angle No. 2 (from the inside at A's neck).

9.   A hits the weapon-bearing arm upwards...

10.   ...and strikes the weapon-bearing arm downwards with his left hand...

11.   ...bringing the knife in such a position so that he can deliver a strike downwards at the head...

12.   ...and strikes using Angle No. 5 (downwards at D's head). D strikes the weapon-bearing arm from the left to the right...

13.   ...controls the weapon-bearing arm with his left hand...

14.   ...and strikes using Angle No. 1 (inwards from the outside at A's neck).

Roles can now be changed over and the Drill begun again!

Drill 3: Fivecount Sumbrada with Disarming

Basics: At the moment the disarming action is carried out, the blade of the person doing the disarming is pointing upwards and the blade of the other person is pointing down to the ground.

Disarming using Angle No. 1 (Knife strike from the outside at the neck)

1. A strikes using Angle No. 1 (from the outside at the neck).
2. D strikes A's right forearm...
3. ...takes hold of the right weapon-bearing arm with his left hand and brings his right arm onto his left hip.
4. D brings the weapon-bearing arm clockwise outwards to the right...
5. ...stretches his right thumb out...
6. ...and clamps the weapon-bearing wrist between his blade and thumb...

7. ...brings the weapon-bearing arm further clockwise outwards to the left, places the left hand on the flat, blunt side of the knife...

8. ...and carries out the disarming action with the left hand.

Disarming using Angle No. 4 (Knife strike from the inside at hip-height)

1. A strikes using Angle No. 4 (from the inside at hip-height).

2. D strikes A's right hand...

3. ...and controls the right hand with his own left hand.

4. When A stretches his right thumb out...

5. ...D clamps the weapon-bearing wrist between his blade and the thumb...

6. ...brings the weapon-bearing hand further clockwise outwards to the left, places the left hand on the flat, blunt side of the knife...

7. ...and carries out the disarming action with the left hand.

Disarming using Angle No. 5 (Knife stab at the stomach)

1. A stabs using Angle No. 5 (at the stomach). D strikes A's right forearm...

2. ...takes hold of A's weapon-bearing wrist with the left hand, stretches his right thumb out...

3. ...clamps the weapon-bearing wrist between his blade and thumb...

4. ...brings the weapon-bearing arm further clockwise outwards to the left, places the left hand on the flat, blunt side of the knife...

5. ...and carries out the disarming action with the left hand.

Disarming using Angle No. 2 (Knife stab from the inside at the neck)

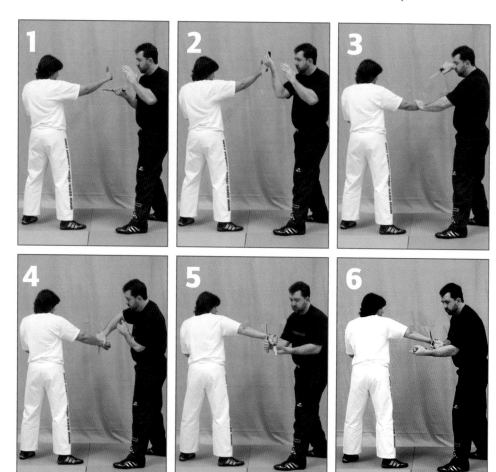

1. A strikes using Angle No. 2 (from the inside at the neck).
2. D strikes the weapon-bearing arm upwards...
3. ...and sweeps the weapon-bearing arm downwards with his left hand. D stretches his right thumb...
4. ...and clamps the weapon-bearing wrist between his blade and thumb...
5. ...brings the weapon-bearing arm further clockwise outwards to the left, places the left hand on the flat, blunt side of the knife...
6. ...and carries out the disarming action with the left hand.

Disarming using Angle No. 5 (Knife strike downwards at the head)

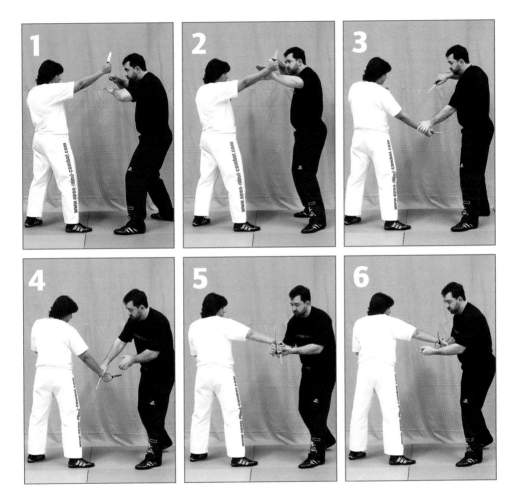

1. A strikes using Angle No. 5 (downwards at the head).
2. D strikes the weapon-bearing arm, sweeps it outwards to the left with the left hand...
3. ...and continues to sweep it with the left hand further counter-clockwise downwards and outwards to the right. When A stretches his right thumb out...
4. ...D clamps the weapon-bearing wrist between his blade and thumb...
5. ...brings the weapon-bearing arm further clockwise outwards to the left, places the left hand on the flat, blunt side of the knife...
6. ...and carries out the disarming action with the left hand.

Drill 4

1. A stabs at the left side of D's chest. With the left hand, D sweeps the weapon-bearing arm inwards...

2. ...and at the same time strikes A's weapon-bearing arm.

3. D stabs at the left side of A's chest. With the left hand, A sweeps the weapon-bearing arm inwards and at the same time strikes D's weapon-bearing arm.

4. With the left hand, A sweeps the weapon-bearing arm further inwards.

5. A strikes using Angle No. 1 (from the outside at the neck).

6. D strikes the weapon-bearing arm and controls it with his left hand...

7. ...and uses Angle No. 4 as a stab towards the liver. With the left hand, A parries the stab.

8. A stabs at the left side of D's chest. With the left hand, D sweeps the weapon-bearing arm inwards and at the same time strikes A's weapon-bearing arm.

9. D strikes using Angle No. 1 (from the outside at the neck). A strikes the weapon-bearing arm...

10. ...controls it with the left hand...

11. ...and delivers Angle No. 4 as a stab towards the liver. With the left hand, D parries the stab.

Drill 5

1. A strikes using Angle No. 1 (inwards from the outside at the neck).
2. With the left hand, D carries out a block with the edge of the hand (palm down block) upwards and outwards to the left and stabs using Angle No. 5 (at the stomach).
3. Because A is very strong, D cannot stop him with the left arm so D rolls round the weapon-bearing arm...
4. ...and, in doing so, brings it clockwise downwards and inwards.
5. Having reached the end of the movement inside, D carries on taking hold of the weapon-bearing arm with his left forearm and stabs once again using Angle No. 5 (at the stomach).

28 Shadowboxing/Currenza

A very effective method for improving the self-defense abilities is to carry out the sequences learned without a partner in a form of "Shadowboxing" (Currenza). It is best to do this in front of a mirror. At the beginning it might be a bit difficult but after a while you will begin to feel success. The trainee visualizes a real situation and carries out the necessary defense techniques. Music, in particular percussion instruments, can be of help in this respect e.g. using the conga drum (Tip: CD Quem & Zaka Percussions). The trainee should adjust himself to the various rhythms and carry out the techniques in harmony with the music.

Appendix

Literature

On my Internet web pages under www.open-mind-combat.com a list of books can be found. Those interested can gain an overview of the Martial Arts literature. The publishers of this book, Meyer & Meyer, have a large coverage of publications on the Martial Arts – see their Internet web page under www.m-m-sports.com

Internet:
www.fight-academy.eu   Fight Academy Christian Braun

Sources for Training Knifes, Sticks and Safety Glasses:

Christian Braun
Peter-Paul-Rubens-Str. 1
67227 Frankenthal
E-Mail: Cristian.Braun@open-mind-combat.com
Internet: www.open-mind-combat.com

Training Address:
Fight Academy Christian Braun
Westendstr. 15
67059 Ludwigshafen
Germany
Cellphone +49 177 28 430 80

Photo & Illustration Credits

Cover Design: Jens Vogelsang
Photos: Jessica Rogall-Zelt

About the Author

Christian Braun
Peter-Paul-Rubens-Str. 1
67227 Frankenthal
E-Mail: Christian.Braun@open-mind-combat.com
Internet: www.open-mind-combat.com

Requests for information regarding courses, books and private training should be sent to the above address.

Qualifications:
* Head Instructor Open Mind Combat (OMC)
* 5th Dan Ju-Jutsu, Licensed JJ-Instructor, Trainer 'B' License
* Phase 6 and Madunong Guro in the IKAEF under Jeff Espinous and Johan Skalberg
* Instructor in Progressive Fighting Systems (Jeet Kune Do Concepts) under Paul Vunak
* Instructor in Luta-Livre License Grade 1 under Andreas Schmidt
* 1st Dan Jiu-Jitsu (German Jiu-Jitsu Association)
* Phase 2 Jun Fan Gung Fu under Ralf Beckmann

Personal Security:
* Trainer for personal security for the managing board of a big IT-Company in Baden-Württemberg, Germany.
* Trainer for personal security of the company MS Event Security in Grünstad, Germany.

Offices held:
* 1990-1991 – Trainer and Press Representative for the Ju-Jutsu Section of the Judo Association for the German State of the Pfalz (Rhineland Palatinate)
* 1999-2003 – Speaker for the Ju-Jutsu Association (Ju-Jutsu Verband Baden e.V.) in matters for Sport for Seniors and the Disabled
* 1992-today – Head of Section in the Turn- und Gefechtclub 1861 e.V. (German Gymnastics and Fencing Club 1861)

Organization:
*   Speaker on the German National Seminar of the DJJV e.V. (German Ju-Jutsu Association) 2003 and 2004
*   Speaker at German National Courses held by the DJJV e.V.
*   Speaker in the faculty of JJ Instructors Division of the DJJV e.V.
*   Member of the Trainer Team of the Ju-Jutsu Verband Baden e.V.
*   Member of the Trainer Team of the DJJV e.V. in the faculty for Sport for the Disabled

Competition Achievements in the Upper Open Weight Classes:
Between 1988-1991 several place results achieved in the Pfalz Individual Championships with 1st Place taken in 1991. Placed in Third Place, three times in the German South-West Individual Championships. 2004, placed in Fourth Place in the Lock and Choke Tournament of the European Luta-Livre-Organization in the Upper Open Weight Class. In January 2005 in Karlsruhe, placed in Second Place in the Submissao Grappling Challenge. In February 2005 in Cologne, placed in Second Place in the Luta-Livre German Individual Championships in the Weight Class +99 kg.

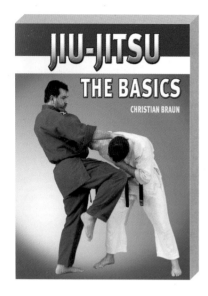

Christian Braun
**Jiu-Jitsu
– The Basics**

In almost a thousand step by step photographs, the Jiu-Jitsu techniques are explained, so that Jiu-Jitsuka of any standard will be able to follow them and use them. Another feature of "Jiu-Jitsu – The Basics" are lessons concerning lokking, throwing, striking and kicking techniques, as well as an introduction to self-defense in groundwork. This book on the basics will also provide the trainer with a comprehensive reference book.

200 pages, full-color print
900 photos and illustrations
Paperback, 5^3/4" x 8^1/4"
ISBN 1-84126-171-8
£ 12.95 UK/$ 17.95 US
$ 25.95 CDN/€ 16.95

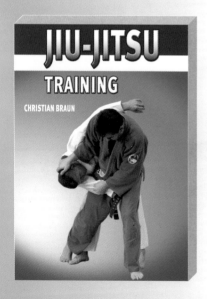

Christian Braun
**Jiu-Jitsu
Training**

Jiu-Jitsu Training moves on from the author's first book, Jiu-Jitsu – The Basics, and is directed at every Jiu-Jitsuka who has learned the basics and wants to improve. In more than a thousand illustrative photographs, the techniques are explained step by step. The book covers the basic positions, techniques and combinations. It Includes an introduction to self-defense in groundwork.
An effective preparation for a grading test and a comprehensive reference book!

264 pages, full-color print
1431 photos and illustrations
Paperback, 6^1/2" x 9^1/4"
ISBN 1-84126-179-3
£ 14.95 UK/$ 19.95 US
$ 26.95 CDN/€ 18.95

MEYER
& MEYER
SPORT

MEYER & MEYER distribution@m-m-sports.com• www.m-m-sports.com